GPU Programming using Rust and CUDA

Exploring Rust's potential in GPU and parallel computing using Rust-CUDA, cuda-oxide, and RustaCUDA

Maris Fenlor

Published by: GitforGits

www.gitforgits.com

Printed in India

First Printing: July 2026

ISBN: 978-93-49174-37-5

Cover Design by: Kitten Publishing

Disclaimer:

This book, including all its text, diagrams, and illustrations, is an original work developed for educational and informational purposes. The content is not affiliated with, endorsed by, or sponsored by or any other company, brand, or entity referenced within. All brand names, product names, and trademarks mentioned are the property of their respective owners and are used in a descriptive, educational context only. Every effort has been made to ensure that no copyrighted or trademarked material has been copied or misused in this book. All diagrams and illustrations that are not original have been used with proper attribution and credit to their respective sources.

If you believe that any content in this book infringes upon your copyright or trademark, please contact us immediately at support@gitforgits.com. Upon notification, corrective action will be taken promptly.

Prologue

There's a general consensus that every technology has a door that's locked. For GPU computing, that doorway has had a sign up for nearly twenty years saying C++ only. I mean, Python found a side entrance by wrapping what C++ built. Usually, everyone else waited outside, and waiting outside became so normal that we stopped noticing the wait.

I wrote this book because I stopped believing the sign.

The Rust system programming language arrived on the scene with a pretty unusual set of promises, **speed without fear**. Its compiler catches memory mistakes and data races that can take years to debug, and it does so before the program even runs. For years, that offer stopped at the edge of the GPU, where thousands of threads shared memory in ways no borrow checker was designed to see. Then the toolchains started to appear. It was a community project that taught the Rust compiler to emit PTX. And NVIDIA's own lab has come up with an experimental compiler that can prove some kernels race-free by type alone. The driver API was wrapped so cleanly in a quiet crate that GPU memory management became boring. And that is the highest compliment systems programmers know how to give!

And this book is great because it takes you through that journey in a really careful and honest way. We're not saying Rust has taken over GPU computing, because it hasn't. We're not going to pretend the experimental toolchains are finished, because they're not, and every chapter labels them clearly. We'll build, run, measure and verify chapter after chapter until the question of whether Rust can do this work stops being a matter of opinion and becomes a matter of record on your own hardware. We'll be writing kernels in Rust and seeing how they match up with their C++ equivalents. If you feed a GPU properly, you'll see bandwidth quadruple from just one changed subscript. It'll get you working with thousands of threads without a single silent race, pricing a financial option based on an exact formula, and shipping an inference pipeline that outruns its Python equivalent for reasons you can name. There's nothing in these chapters that asks for your trust. It seems like every app out there is trying to get your keyboard.

I'd also like to say something about who I imagine holding this book. It's like when you write parallel code in C++ and you're wondering what the borrow checker would change. Maybe you're writing Rust and the GPU feels like someone else's territory. It's like you came from Python, loving how comfortable it is and wanting to know what's going on under the surface. The three of you will find the same thing here, one growing workspace, one honest benchmark protocol, and one repeated discovery, which is that the exotic machinery of GPU computing becomes ordinary engineering once a language finally tells you the truth about your own code.

--Maris Fenlor

Contents

Preface

C++ has been the go-to for GPU programming for almost 20 years. Well, this book asks a fairly practical question: can Rust do the job, and how well?

This book is all about getting hands-on with different toolchains that connect Rust to NVIDIA hardware. There's RustaCUDA for safe host-side control, the Rust-CUDA project for writing kernels in pure Rust, and NVIDIA's experimental cuda-oxide compiler with its typed launches and async execution graphs. We're going to build one Cargo workspace that keeps on growing. It'll include device queries, launch planning, Rust-written kernels, memory optimization, parallel reductions and scans, multi-stream pipelines, matrix multiplication benchmarked against cuBLAS, a Monte Carlo option pricer validated against a closed formula, and a complete batched inference application measured against a Python baseline.

We'll check every result against a CPU reference, and the reports will give accurate numbers, including where libraries outperform hand-written kernels and where experimental toolchains are still a work in progress. After that, we'll look at working profiling skills using Nsight Systems, Nsight Compute, and Compute Sanitizer.

In this book you will learn to:

- Launch, synchronize, and verify GPU kernels with ownership-managed device memory.
- Write real CUDA kernels using Rust-CUDA and cuda-oxide.
- Plan grids, blocks, and warps for 2D workloads.
- Accelerate transfer speeds with pinned memory and coalesced access patterns.
- Build race-free thread cooperation using shared memory, barriers, and atomics.
- Overlap transfers with computation using streams, events, and async Rust pipelines.
- Optimize matrix multiplication and benchmark against cuBLAS ceiling.
- Wrap CUDA C library safely with handles, error enums, and Drop.
- Ship complete batched GPU inference application against Python baselines.
- Diagnose performance with Nsight Systems, Nsight Compute, and compute-sanitizer.

GitforGits

Prerequisites

The book is meant for people who work with parallel programming, developers who are just starting out with GPU work, and CUDA programmers who are curious about Rust. All you need is some basic Rust knowledge, a Linux machine, and an NVIDIA GPU. It doesn't matter if you've never used CUDA C++ before.

Codes Usage

Are you in need of some helpful code examples to assist you in your programming and documentation? Look no further! Our book offers a wealth of supplemental material, including code examples and exercises.

Not only is this book here to aid you in getting your job done, but you have our permission to use the example code in your programs and documentation. However, please note that if you are reproducing a significant portion of the code, we do require you to contact us for permission.

But don't worry, using several chunks of code from this book in your program or answering a question by citing our book and quoting example code does not require permission. But if you do choose to give credit, an attribution typically includes the title, author, publisher, and ISBN. For example, "GPU Programming using Rust and CUDA by Maris Fenlor".

If you are unsure whether your intended use of the code examples falls under fair use or the permissions outlined above, please do not hesitate to reach out to us at support@gitforgits.com.

We are happy to assist and clarify any concerns.

Acknowledgement

I owe a tremendous debt of gratitude to GitforGits, for their unflagging enthusiasm and wise counsel throughout the entire process of writing this book. Their knowledge and careful editing helped make sure the piece was useful for people of all reading levels and comprehension skills. In addition, I'd like to thank everyone involved in the publishing process for their efforts in making this book a reality. Their efforts, from copyediting to advertising, made the project what it is today.

Finally, I'd like to express my gratitude to everyone who has shown me unconditional love and encouragement throughout my life. Their support was crucial to the completion of this book. I appreciate your help with this endeavor and your continued interest in my career.

CHAPTER 1

NEW BENEFICIARY OF GPU COMPUTING

In this chapter, we will set up everything our GPU work needs and confirm that a Rust program can see, question, and describe the graphics card inside our Linux machine. At the very beginning, we will try to place Rust honestly within the GPU computing landscape, where C++ has ruled for nearly two decades and where Python has become the approachable front desk. We will then survey the three toolchains that make Rust on CUDA possible today, namely Rust-CUDA, cuda-oxide, and RustaCUDA, and we will label the maturity of each so that our expectations stay realistic throughout the book.

After the survey, we will prepare our laboratory. We will verify the NVIDIA driver, install the CUDA Toolkit on Linux, and add the Rust toolchain pieces that GPU work demands. We will then create **`gpu_lab`**, the Cargo workspace that will grow with us across every chapter of this book. Our first member of that workspace will be a small device query program that interrogates the GPU and prints its name, memory size, and compute capability. As this chapter closes, we will have a verified, repeatable environment and the confidence that Rust truly converses with CUDA hardware.

Dominance of C++

For almost two decades, one language has controlled the doorway to serious GPU computing. When NVIDIA released CUDA in 2007, it arrived as an extension of C and C++, and every kernel, every optimization manual, and every code sample that followed reinforced that choice. In 2008, Nickolls, Buck, Garland, and Skadron formalized this single source CPU and GPU model in their ACM Queue paper, Scalable Parallel Programming with CUDA, and the model they presented remains the industry default today. Our book asks a simple question about that doorway:

Can Rust walk through it and feel at home?

C++ Stronghold

The dominance of C++ in GPU work is easy to explain. First, NVIDIA built the CUDA Toolkit around **`nvcc`**, a compiler that blends host and device code in one translation unit, and then surrounded it with profilers, debuggers, and libraries such as cuBLAS and cuFFT. The official CUDA C++ programming documentation at **docs.nvidia.com** remains the reference point for every GPU practitioner, whatever language they prefer. With that gravity, teams standardized on C++ because the vendor kept that road paved, lit, and patrolled, while every alternative remained gravel.

The stronghold, however, collects a toll. Within that stronghold, raw pointers have long traveled between host and device with no ownership rules attached, and a mistaken size in a single memcpy can corrupt results silently rather than loudly. Meanwhile, the data races between threads compiles without complaint, and use after free bugs surface only under load. None of these failures are exotic in daily CUDA work, and each one costs hours of tracing. The Rust language was designed to target exactly these categories of failure, which is why its arrival in GPU computing deserves a serious trial rather than a shrug.

Python's Convenience Layer

Meanwhile, Python became the approachable front desk of GPU computing without ever writing a kernel of its own. Through libraries such as PyTorch, CuPy, and Numba, millions of developers move data to the GPU with a single line, while compiled C++ and CUDA code performs the actual work behind the curtain. This arrangement is productive and pleasant, and we will use it later in this book as a benchmark partner.

However, such arrangement also had edges, because performance falls off sharply the moment a workload steps outside the prebuilt library paths. When such moment arrives, a Python developer must drop into CUDA C++ anyway and must carry all the risks we described above. A deployment story built on interpreters and virtual environments also travels poorly to embedded devices and latency sensitive services. Our interest in Rust begins precisely here. If Rust can match Python's day-to-day comfort for routine GPU tasks while producing a single static binary with native performance, then it earns a real seat at the table rather than a guest pass.

Entry of Rust

The Rust language brings assets that map naturally onto GPU programming pain. Its ownership model catches entire classes of memory misuse before anything runs, its **`Result`** values turn every CUDA error code into something we must handle, and RAII releases device memory the instant a value goes out of scope. The Rust CUDA project documentation at **rust-gpu.github.io/rust-cuda** adds a subtle performance point as well, because Rust's aliasing rules give every kernel the benefit that C++ programmers only get when they annotate pointers by hand with **`__restrict__`**.

I also want to be very clear and honest about what this book does not claim. We are not announcing that Rust has conquered GPU computing, and we are not asking anyone to abandon a working C++ codebase. Our purpose is exploratory. We will run the code on the hardware, and you shall experience the result. Where a toolchain is experimental, we will say so at that moment itself. And, if a library outperforms our handwritten kernels, I will show you the numbers and recommend the library right away with complete confidence.

Rust's GPU Toolchains Today

We can count three toolchains that currently connect Rust to CUDA, and each one occupies a different position on the risk and reward map:

1. With RustaCUDA, we gain stable, safe control over the GPU from the host side.
2. The Rust-CUDA project lets us write the kernels themselves in Rust through a dedicated compiler backend.

3. Finally, cuda-oxide, an experimental compiler from NVIDIA's own labs, pushes furthest with typed kernel launches and async execution graphs.

We will work with all three in this book. We will explore each one properly in the following:

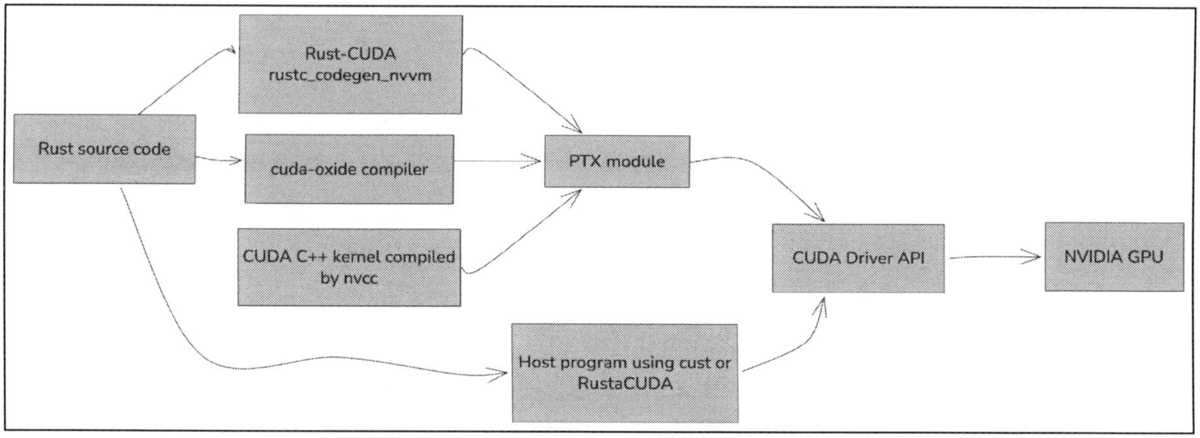

Fig 1.1: Rust to CUDA Toolchain Landscape

Rust-CUDA Project

The Rust-CUDA project aims to make Rust a first-class language for CUDA work, and its centerpiece is **`rustc_codegen_nvvm`**, a compiler backend that translates Rust into NVVM IR for NVIDIA's libnvvm library, which then emits optimized PTX. Around that backend sit two companion crates:

1. The **`cuda_std`** crate supplies device side utilities such as thread index queries,
2. while **`cust`** wraps the CUDA Driver API on the host side with RAII types and **`Result`** based errors.

There is detailed project documentation at **rust-gpu.github.io/rust-cuda** describes this architecture in full detail.

Historically, this road was rocky, because the older LLVM PTX backend generated invalid PTX for many common Rust operations, and earlier efforts such as accel and nvptx stalled for that reason. The project now lives under the wider Rust GPU umbrella, and its team maintains it actively, though it still requires a specific nightly Rust toolchain and careful setup. We will treat it as our primary vehicle for writing kernels in pure Rust when we reach a later chapter, and we will keep its experimental nature visible whenever we depend on it.

cuda-oxide

With cuda-oxide, the NVIDIA's NVlabs team offers a second route to the same destination. This experimental compiler turns standard Rust into PTX with no DSL and no foreign bindings, and it adds conveniences such as the **`#[cuda_module]`** attribute, typed launch methods generated per kernel, and the bounds checked `DisjointSlice` type for device memory. Its most distinctive idea is the `DeviceOperation` model, which composes GPU work as lazy graphs that async Rust can await. The cuda-oxide book at **nvlabs.github.io/cuda-oxide** documents every feature we will rely upon.

At the time of writing, the cuda-oxide sits at version 0.1.0, and its authors describe the release as an early alpha with expected bugs and API breakage. We will use only the features that its published documentation demonstrates end to end, namely typed launches, bounds checked slices, and the async pipeline pattern. We will keep the speculative capabilities or features out of our plan for now, because I believe that overpromises on alpha software is of no help to any programmer. So, in later chapters, we will put this toolchain to work.

RustaCUDA

In contrast to the two compilers, RustaCUDA solves a smaller problem and solves it with reassuring stability. This crate, created by Brook Heisler, wraps the CUDA Driver API in safe, ergonomic Rust and gives us contexts, modules, streams, and device memory as ordinary owned values. It compiles on stable Rust, needs nothing beyond the CUDA libraries themselves, and happily launches any PTX we hand it, whichever compiler produced that PTX. The API reference at **docs.rs/rustacuda** walks through every module we will touch later.

This modesty of scope is precisely what makes RustaCUDA the calmest place to begin. Because the crate never attempts to compile our Rust into GPU code, nothing about it depends on nightly toolchains, patched backends, or alpha releases, and a project built on it today will still build the same way a year from now. We will therefore start our hands-on work later with RustaCUDA, so that our first launches, transfers, and synchronization habits form on ground that does not shift beneath us while we are still finding our footing.

Setting up Lab

To learn and practice well, the best option for me would be Linux with an NVIDIA GPU.

Verifying Driver

The kernel driver is the one component that everything else depends on, so we will confirm it before touching anything Rust related. Almost every Linux distribution will offer NVIDIA's proprietary driver through its standard package manager, and cloud GPU images usually arrive with it preinstalled and preconfigured. A quick interrogation tells us whether the driver is alive and which CUDA version it can serve.

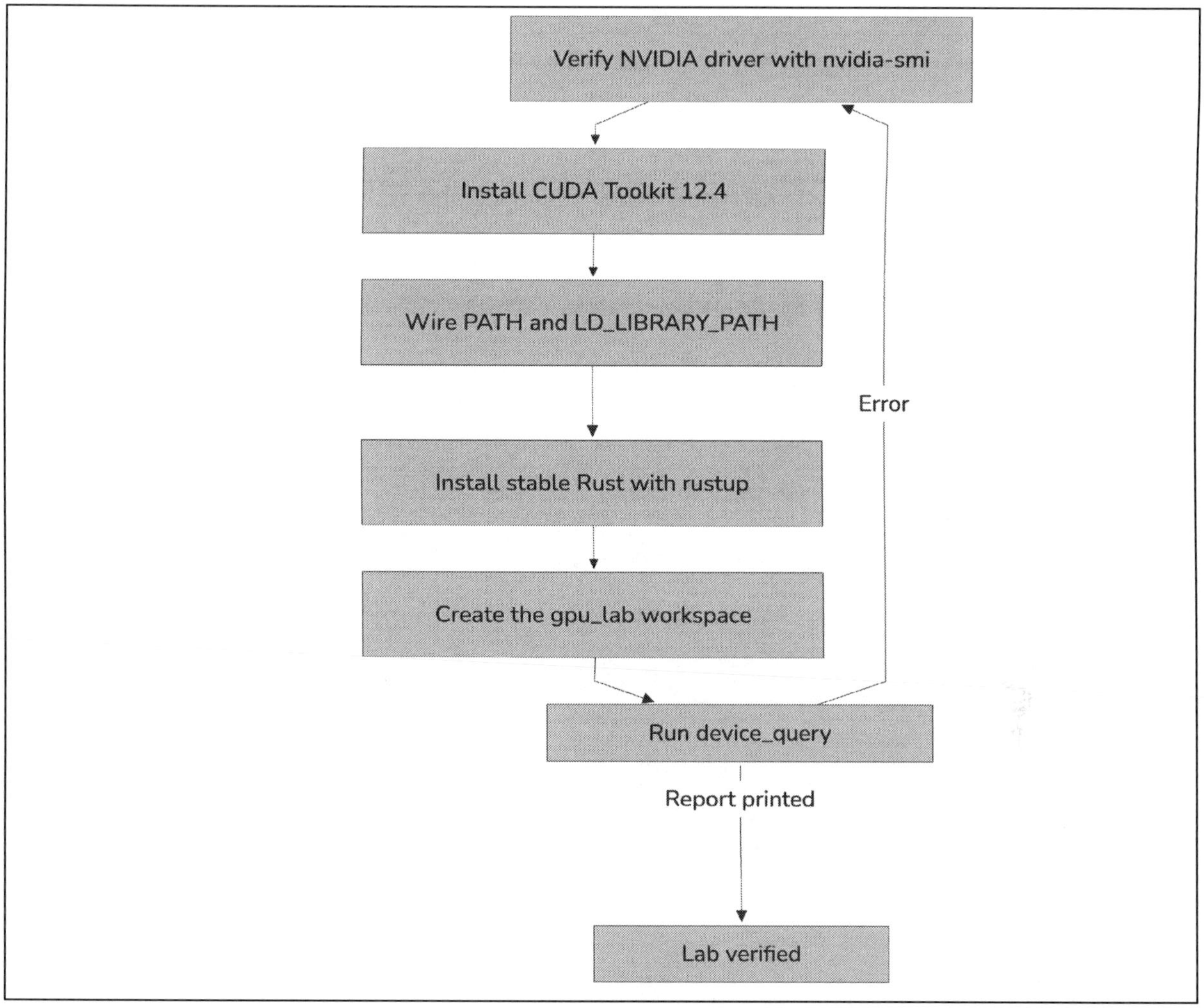

Fig 1.2: Lab Setup

So here, we will ask the driver to introduce itself with the nvidia-smi utility:

```
nvidia-smi
```

This thing replies with a table naming our GPU, and the two fields we care about sit in the top row:

```
+-----------------------------------------------------------------------------+
| NVIDIA-SMI 550.54.15    Driver Version: 550.54.15    CUDA Version: 12.4
|
|   0  NVIDIA GeForce RTX 3080        On  | 00000000:01:00.0  Off              |
+-----------------------------------------------------------------------------+
```

The Driver Version field confirms that the kernel module is loaded and speaking to the hardware. The CUDA Version field is frequently misread, because it does not report an installed toolkit at all. Instead, it states the newest CUDA release this driver can support, which gives us an upper bound for the toolkit we are about to install.

If the command fails or reports no devices, the driver needs attention first, and NVIDIA's Linux driver instructions at docs.nvidia.com resolve the common cases before anything else in this chapter can proceed.

Installing CUDA Toolkit

With the driver confirmed, we can now add the CUDA Toolkit, which supplies the compiler, headers, libraries, and profiling tools that our Rust crates will link against. Helpfully, the NVIDIA versions the toolkit and the driver independently, so a 12.4 toolkit runs happily under any driver that reports 12.4 or newer. For each distribution, NVIDIA publishes a dedicated package repository, and the official Linux installation reference at **docs.nvidia.com/cuda** lists the exact variant for every release.

So here, we will register NVIDIA's repository and install the toolkit as below:

```
wget
https://developer.download.nvidia.com/compute/cuda/repos/ubuntu2204/x86_64
/cuda-keyring_1.1-1_all.deb

sudo dpkg -i cuda-keyring_1.1-1_all.deb

sudo apt-get update

sudo apt-get -y install cuda-toolkit-12-4
```

Once the packages settle, the compiler and libraries live under **`/usr/local/cuda`**, but our shell does not know about that location yet. A pair of environment variables will complete the wiring. The first extends the executable search path, and the second tells the loader where the CUDA shared libraries reside. We will place both in **`.bashrc`** so that every future session inherits them without ceremony, and a missed export at this point is the single most common cause of mysterious build failures later.

So now, we will append both lines and reload the configuration:

```
echo 'export PATH=/usr/local/cuda/bin:$PATH' >> ~/.bashrc

echo 'export LD_LIBRARY_PATH=/usr/local/cuda/lib64:$LD_LIBRARY_PATH' >>
~/.bashrc

source ~/.bashrc
```

We then ask the freshly installed compiler to identify itself:

```
nvcc --version
```

The reply then names the release and settles that the toolkit is in place:

```
nvcc: NVIDIA (R) Cuda compiler driver
Cuda compilation tools, release 12.4, V12.4.131
```

Preparing Rust Toolchain

Our Rust installation follows the standard rustup route, which keeps multiple toolchains side by side and will matter later when a kernel compiler pins a specific nightly build. For now, stable Rust is all this chapter needs, because RustaCUDA and **cust** both compile on stable. If rustup already manages the machine, a quick **rustup update** brings everything current and nothing else changes.

```
curl --proto '=https' --tlsv1.2 -sSf https://sh.rustup.rs | sh
source "$HOME/.cargo/env"
```

We will run a quick version check as well:

```
cargo --version
```

```
cargo 1.88.0 (873a06493 2025-05-10)
```

Creating Project

Every chapter of this book contributes code to one growing Cargo workspace named **gpu_lab**, so nothing we build is a throwaway. A workspace suits GPU work particularly well, because later chapters will separate host crates from kernel crates while they share one target directory and one lockfile.

Our first member is **device_query**, the program that will interrogate the GPU in the next section.

Here, we will create the workspace root together with its first member:

```
mkdir gpu_lab && cd gpu_lab
cargo new device_query
```

We then declare the workspace in a root Cargo.toml as below:

```
[workspace]
members = ["device_query"]
resolver = "2"
```

After this, our directory holds a root manifest and one member crate, and **cargo build** at the root compiles every member in a single pass. Each future chapter will add members beside **device_query**, such as the kernels crate later and the pipeline crate later, and the shared target directory keeps rebuild times short as the family grows. This arrangement also mirrors how production Rust teams organize multi crate systems, so the habits we practice here transfer directly to real projects beyond this book.

First Contact with GPU

Device Query Program

Our first Rust conversation with the GPU uses **cust**, the host side crate from the Rust-CUDA project. We choose it over RustaCUDA for this opening program for one practical reason, namely that **cust** is the crate we will keep using when our own Rust kernels arrive later, so meeting it early pays forward. On stable Rust, it needs only the driver we already verified, and no kernel compiler is involved anywhere.

So now, we will declare the dependency in **device_query/Cargo.toml**:

```
[dependencies]
cust = "0.3"
```

The program itself fits in one file and exercises the three ideas this chapter promised, namely initialization, device discovery, and attribute queries. Every fallible call returns a **Result**, so the question mark operator threads any CUDA error cleanly out of **main** instead of crashing us somewhere in the middle. If you could notice here, that nothing in this file carries an **unsafe** marker, because querying a device involves no kernel launches and no raw memory, and **cust** exposes that entire surface as safe Rust.

Next, we will replace the contents of **device_query/src/main.rs** with the following code:

```
use cust::device::{Device, DeviceAttribute};
use cust::CudaFlags;

fn main() -> Result<(), Box<dyn std::error::Error>> {
    cust::init(CudaFlags::empty())?;
    println!("CUDA driver initialized.");

    let device_total = Device::num_devices()?;
    println!("Detected {} CUDA device(s).", device_total);
```

```
    let device = Device::get_device(0)?;
    println!("Name: {}", device.name()?);
    println!(
        "Total memory: {} MB",
        device.total_memory()? / (1024 * 1024)
    );
    println!(
        "Streaming multiprocessors: {}",
        device.get_attribute(DeviceAttribute::MultiprocessorCount)?
    );
    println!(
        "Compute capability: {}.{}",
        device.get_attribute(DeviceAttribute::ComputeCapabilityMajor)?,
        device.get_attribute(DeviceAttribute::ComputeCapabilityMinor)?
    );

    Ok(())
}
```

Now here, I want you to have a closer look before we run anything. In the above, the **cust::init** call loads and initializes the CUDA driver, and every later operation depends on it, which is why it stands first and why its failure ends the program immediately with a readable error. The **Device::get_device** call hands us a lightweight handle rather than a live connection, so no context exists yet and no device memory has been touched. And then, there are attribute queries such as **MultiprocessorCount** read static facts the driver already knows, so the whole program stays quick and harmless on any machine.

Reading GPU

From the workspace root, we will now build and run our first member:

```
cargo run -p device_query
```

On our reference machine, the GPU introduces itself like this:

```
CUDA driver initialized.
Detected 1 CUDA device(s).
```

```
Name: NVIDIA GeForce RTX 3080
Total memory: 10240 MB
Streaming multiprocessors: 68
Compute capability: 8.6
```

From the above output, each line is going to make sense in later chapters. So, you must read it properly now. The memory figure bounds how much data we can park on the device at once, a limit later work runs up against directly. The streaming multiprocessor figure tells us how many independent processors will execute our thread blocks, which shapes the grid sizing decisions we make from chapter 2 onward. The compute capability names the hardware generation, and both kernel compilers use it to decide which PTX features they may emit for this specific GPU.

With that, our lab is good. We have so far verified the driver, installed the toolkit, prepared stable Rust, and watched a Rust binary interrogate real CUDA hardware through nothing more exotic than a crate dependency. We can confidently say, that the **`gpu_lab`** workspace now exists, and it will accompany us to the final chapter while it gains a new member almost every time, we learn something new. In the next chapter, we will slow down and acquire the CUDA execution model itself, because every launch decision we make afterward rests on how grids, blocks, and threads map onto the hardware we just met.

Chapter 2
Thinking in Threads

In this chapter, we will acquire the mental model that every GPU decision in this book rests upon. We will begin with the strict separation between host and device, two processors with two memories that share nothing by default. We will meet the organizational units CUDA uses to manage work, namely contexts, modules, streams, and functions, and we will climb the thread hierarchy of grids, blocks, and warps. Along the way, we will keep translating each idea into Rust vocabulary, so the concepts arrive wearing the types we already know. Your and my hands are going to stay on the keyboard throughout the book from here.

We will extend the **`gpu_lab`** workspace from chapter 1 with a new member named **`grid_planner`**, a program that reads the hardware limits of our GPU and computes sensible launch shapes for realistic workloads in one and two dimensions. We will write no kernel in this chapter, and that restraint is deliberate, because launch decisions made without this model are guesses. As the chapter closes, we will read a phrase such as 4096 blocks of 256 threads and know exactly what the hardware will do with it.

Host and Device

Two Processors, Two Memories

The first habit we must acquire is to treat our program as a conversation between two separate computers. The host is the CPU with its system RAM, and the device is the GPU with its own onboard memory. The two processors can never dereference each other's pointers, and every byte that crosses between them travels over the PCIe bus at a bandwidth far below what either memory offers locally. The CUDA C++ programming documentation at docs.nvidia.com opens with this separation for good reason, because most beginner confusion traces back to forgetting it.

Some numbers make the separation vivid. A modern GPU reads its own memory at several hundred gigabytes per second, and the RTX 3080 in our reference machine advertises 760 of them, while a PCIe 4.0 x16 link delivers roughly 32 gigabytes per second in each direction. The hardware specifications at nvidia.com publish both figures for every card. The gap of more than twenty to one means a transferred byte must earn its passage, a theme that returns with force later. This separation explains a pattern we will see in every chapter ahead. A Rust **`Vec`** lives in host memory, so the GPU cannot touch it directly, and a device buffer lives in GPU memory, so our CPU code cannot index into it. In fact, Rust sharpens this distinction better than C++ does, because our device allocations will carry their own types, and the compiler will refuse code that confuses the two worlds. What C++ leaves to naming conventions and discipline, Rust promotes into the type system.

Round Trip Every Program Makes

Every GPU program in existence, whatever its language, performs the same round trip. We allocate space on the device, copy input data across, run computation on thousands of threads, and copy results back to the host. The sequence appears in Fig 2.1, and we should read it closely now because each arrow costs time. For now, this plain sequence is our anchor.

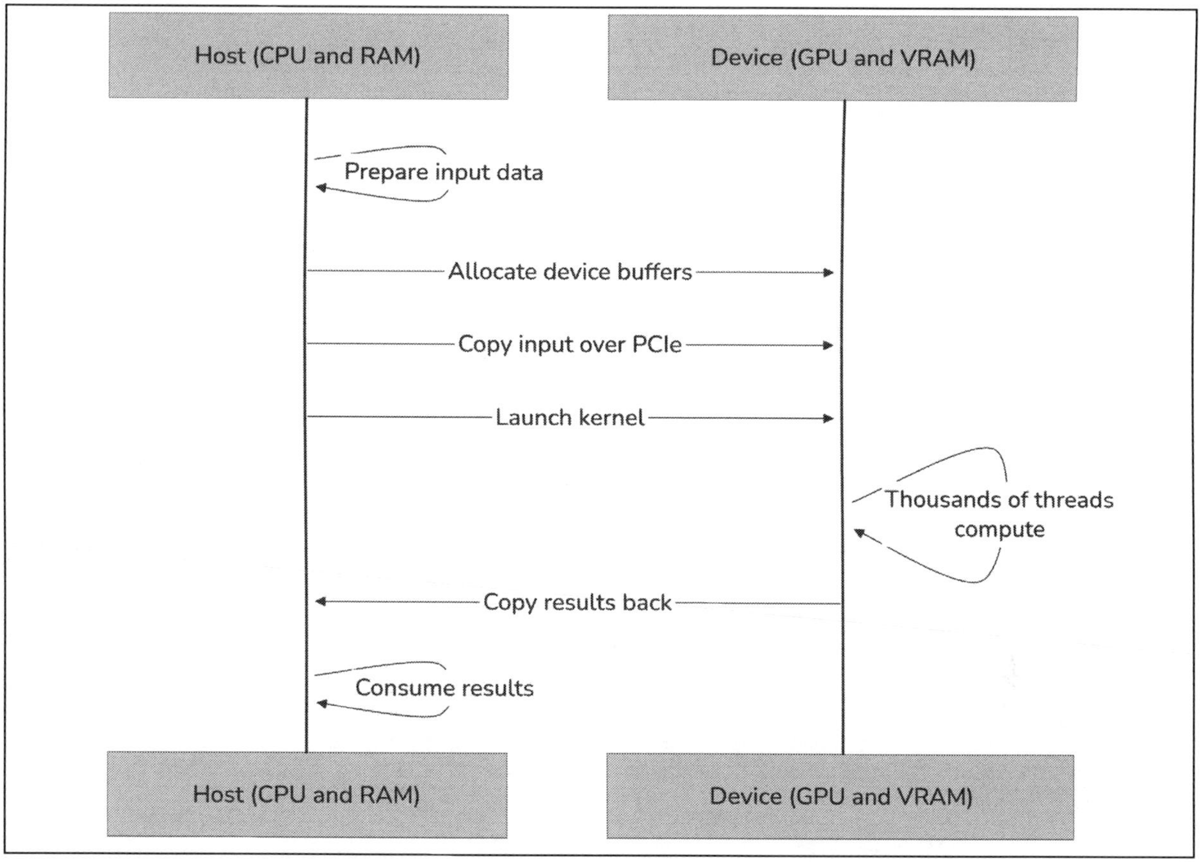

Fig 2.1: Host and Device Round Trip

A useful habit is to read this above diagram with a stopwatch in mind rather than as mere bookkeeping. The two copy arrows cross the slow PCIe link we just measured, while the compute arrow runs at the device's full internal speed, so the profitable programs are the ones that make the middle arrow long and the crossing arrows short. Whenever a GPU port disappoints in practice, the cause is usually a round trip performed too often for too little work per visit, and this one picture is the fastest way to diagnose it.

CUDA's Organizational Units

With the two worlds separated, we can now name the machinery CUDA provides for managing them. We will lean on four units that organize everything, and the RustaCUDA terminology reference at **docs.rs/rustacuda** introduces them with analogies we will adopt because they hold up well in practice. A context resembles a process, a module resembles a shared library, a stream resembles a thread, and a function is a callable kernel. Their relationships form a small data model, and we will keep it in view as the following entity diagram:

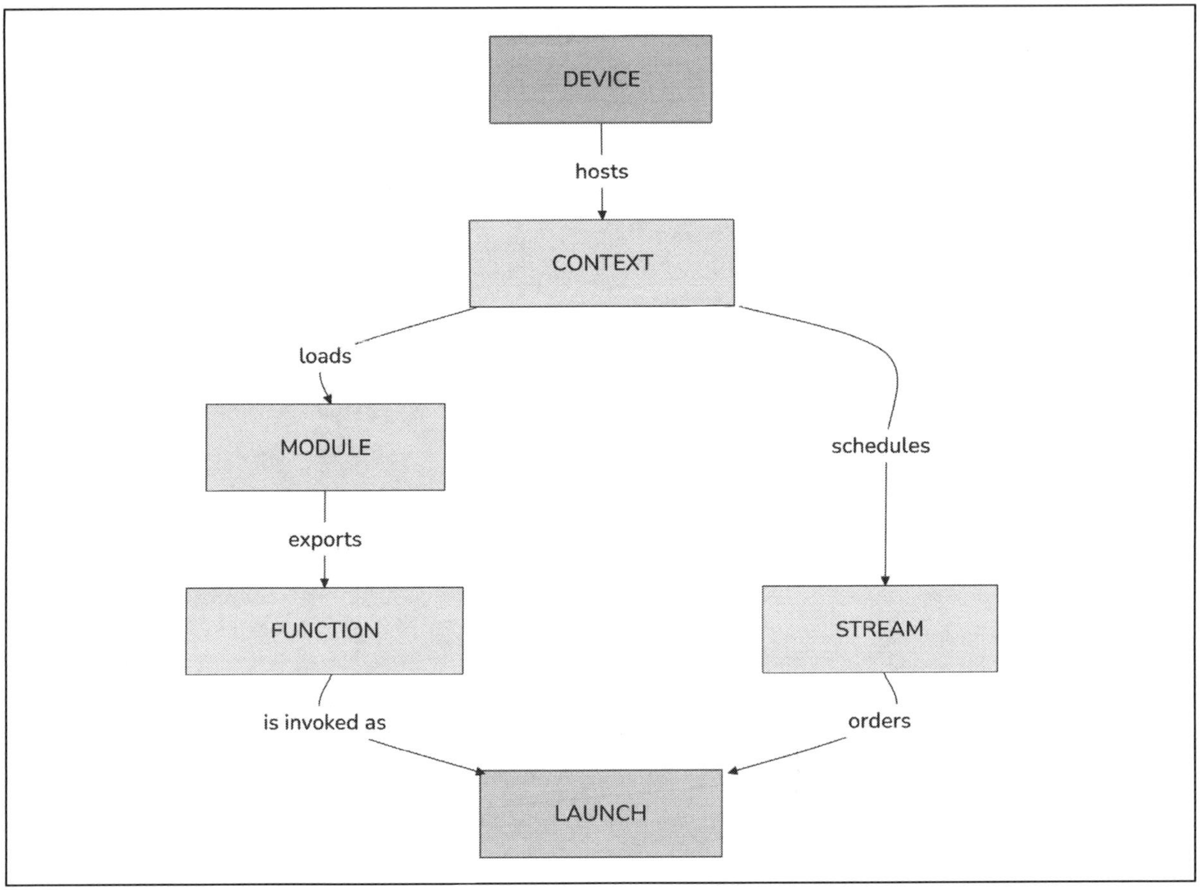

Fig 2.2: Relation between Contexts, Modules, Streams, and Functions

Contexts as GPU Processes

A context owns every piece of state our program creates on a device, such as memory allocations, loaded modules, and streams. When a context dies, everything inside it dies with it, exactly as an operating system reclaims a finished process. Each context binds to a single device, and one program may hold several contexts across several GPUs. In cust, a context is just an ordinary owned value returned by **`context::new`**, and we will watch one live and die inside our program shortly. At no point will it require manual teardown calls.

The process analogy also tells us how many contexts to create, and the comfortable answer is one per device for the whole program. Because every allocation and module belong to the context that made it, two contexts on the same GPU cannot see each other's memory, and juggling several of them multiplies bookkeeping without adding speed. Our chapters therefore create a single context near the top of **`main`** and let it live until the program ends, which keeps ownership obvious and gives **`Drop`** one clean moment to reclaim everything.

Modules as Loadable Libraries

A module is compiled GPU code, packaged as PTX or a binary, that a context loads at runtime. The comparison to a shared object library is precise, because a module export named functions and global values the way a **.so** file exports symbols. This late binding is a gift for our purposes, since the host program does not care which compiler produced the PTX it loads. In the next chapter, we exploit exactly that freedom when our Rust host runs a kernel built elsewhere, and later we swap in PTX that Rust itself produced.

A module load involves more than reading a file. When we hand PTX to the driver, it just in time compiles that portable assembly into the native instruction set of our exact GPU, and it caches the result so later runs skip the work. The compute capability our **device_query** program printed in the previous chapter is precisely what steers this translation. This is why PTX built years ago still runs on hardware that did not exist at the time, a portability trick borrowed from the managed language world.

Streams as Ordered Queues

A stream is a queue of work that the device consumes in submission order. Within one stream, operations run sequentially, and a kernel launched after a copy will wait for that copy to finish. When streams differ, however, the device stays free to interleave and overlap work, which is where real performance lives. For this chapter and the next few, one stream suffices, and we will reach for several of them later when we start hiding transfer time behind computation.

One stream exists before we create any, and CUDA calls it the default stream. Any work submitted without a named stream lands there, which is why simple programs appear to need no streams at all. The default stream also carries an extra synchronizing behavior with respect to the others, and that subtlety trips up many migrating C++ programmers. We will sidestep the trap entirely when we name our streams explicitly from the next chapter onward, a habit both **cust** and RustaCUDA encourage through their APIs.

Functions as Unit of Execution

A function, universally called a kernel, is what actually runs on the device. We load it from a module by name, and we launch it with a shape, which is a grid of blocks of threads chosen per launch rather than per compilation. The launch itself will be our first encounter with unsafe in the next chapter, because at that boundary Rust hands arguments to foreign code it cannot verify. All that lies before that boundary, together with all the machinery in this chapter, will stay inside safe Rust.

A detail worth settling now is how we find a kernel inside its module, because the connection runs on names rather than types. When we ask a module for a function, we pass the exported symbol as a string, and the driver either returns a handle or reports that no such export exists. This lookup happens at runtime, so a misspelled name becomes a polite **Result** error rather than a compile failure, and we will meet exactly that experience in the next chapter. The typed launches of cuda-oxide later exist to close this very gap.

Thread Hierarchy

We now reach the vocabulary that GPU practitioners use daily, and we will need it in every remaining chapter of this book. In CUDA, execution forms a hierarchy with three levels. The threads perform the work, the blocks group threads that may cooperate, and the grid holds every block belonging to one launch.

In the following Fig 2.3, we can think of the shape for a launch we will plan later in this chapter, and the structure reads naturally as an organizational chart:

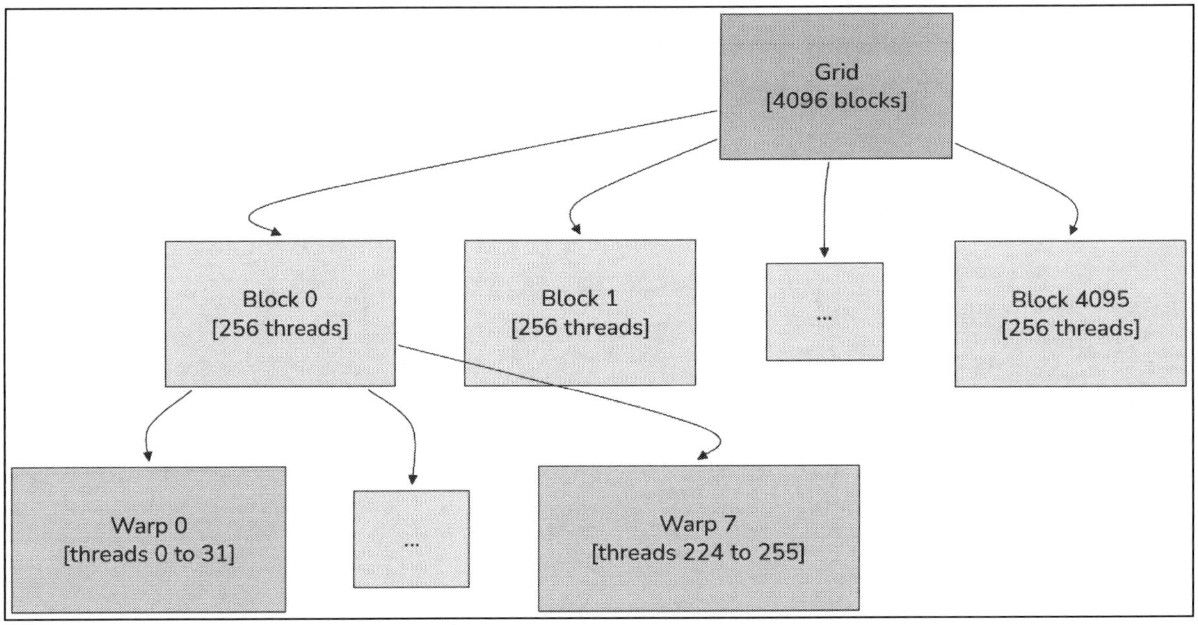

Fig 2.3: One Launch as Organizational Chart

Threads, Blocks, and Grids

Each thread runs the same kernel code with its own identity, and that identity is the mechanism by which one program processes millions of elements. Meanwhile, the blocks group threads into teams of up to 1024, and the threads of one block may share fast on-chip memory and synchronize with one another, an ability a later chapter builds reductions upon. The grid then collects every block of the launch. We may declare both blocks and grids as one, two, or three dimensional, which keeps index arithmetic pleasant when the data itself is an image or a volume.

The hardware assigns whole blocks to streaming multiprocessors, the independent processors our **`device_query`** program reported in the previous chapter, and each SM executes many blocks concurrently when resources allow. Therefore, the blocks must remain independent of one another, because CUDA promises nothing about which SM runs a block or in what order. This independence is what lets the same program scale from a laptop GPU with a handful of SMs to a datacenter card with well over a hundred.

Warps

Under the hood, we find that an SM never executes threads individually. It drives them in groups of 32 called warps, and every thread in a warp executes the same instruction in the same cycle, a model NVIDIA calls SIMT. In their 2008 IEEE Micro paper, NVIDIA Tesla: A Unified Graphics and Computing Architecture, Lindholm, Nickolls, Oberman, and Montrym presented this design, and the warp width of 32 has held across every generation since. When threads of one warp disagree about a branch, the hardware runs both sides serially, so divergence quietly halves throughput.

The warp model also explains why GPUs want far more threads than they have cores. When a warp stalls on a memory access that takes hundreds of cycles, the SM simply switches to another resident warp in a single cycle, and computation continues. This latency hiding only works when enough warps are resident, which is why our launches will routinely oversubscribe the hardware by large factors. The CUDA C++ programming documentation quantifies this idea as occupancy, and a later chapter will let us measure it on our own kernels.

Choosing Sizes

The sizing of a launch is a daily task, and a simple recipe covers most of it. We pick a block size that is a multiple of the warp width, with 128, 256, and 512 as the everyday candidates, and we compute the number of blocks as the ceiling division of elements by block size. The last block usually overhangs the data, so kernels guard with a bounds check, a pattern we will meet later. Helpfully, NVIDIA's best practices material at docs.nvidia.com echoes this recipe almost word for word.

In practice, the data frequently arrives with two dimensions, and the hierarchy handles that shape natively. For a Full HD image of 1920 by 1080 pixels, we can declare blocks of 16 by 16 threads, which multiplies out to 256 threads and keeps our warp multiple intact. The grid then needs 120 blocks across and 68 blocks down, with each dimension computed through the same ceiling division we already trust. Every pixel receives one thread, index arithmetic stays readable, and nothing about the recipe changed except its dimensionality.

To make both recipes concrete, we will now grow our workspace. We will repeat the same steps we used for **`device_query`** in chapter 1, add a member named **`grid_planner`**, list it in the root manifest, and give it the same single **`cust`** dependency. The program asks the driver for the limits that constrain every launch shape, and it then plans launches for one million elements and for a Full HD image.

```
use cust::context::Context;

use cust::device::{Device, DeviceAttribute};
```

```
use cust::CudaFlags;

fn blocks_for(elements: u32, block_size: u32) -> u32 {
    elements.div_ceil(block_size)
}

fn main() -> Result<(), Box<dyn std::error::Error>> {
    cust::init(CudaFlags::empty())?;
    let device = Device::get_device(0)?;
    let _context = Context::new(device)?;
    println!("Context ready on {}.", device.name()?);

    let warp = device.get_attribute(DeviceAttribute::WarpSize)?;
    let max_threads =
device.get_attribute(DeviceAttribute::MaxThreadsPerBlock)?;
    let max_grid_x = device.get_attribute(DeviceAttribute::MaxGridDimX)?;
    let sm_total =
device.get_attribute(DeviceAttribute::MultiprocessorCount)?;

    println!("Warp size: {}", warp);
    println!("Max threads per block: {}", max_threads);
    println!("Max grid dimension x: {}", max_grid_x);
    println!("Streaming multiprocessors: {}", sm_total);

    let elements: u32 = 1_048_576;
    for block_size in [128u32, 256, 512] {
        let grid = blocks_for(elements, block_size);
        println!(
            "{} elements -> {} blocks of {} threads ({} blocks per SM)",
            elements,
            grid,
            block_size,
            grid / sm_total as u32
        );
```

```
    }

    let (width, height) = (1920u32, 1080u32);
    let (bx, by) = (16u32, 16u32);
    println!(
        "{}x{} image -> grid {}x{} of {}x{} blocks",
        width,
        height,
        blocks_for(width, bx),
        blocks_for(height, by),
        bx,
        by
    );

    match Device::get_device(99) {
        Ok(d) => println!("Unexpected device: {}", d.name()?),
        Err(e) => println!("Device 99 refused politely: {}", e),
    }

    Ok(())
}
```

Now here, there are two details in this file that deserves immediate attention:

1. The **blocks_for** helper performs ceiling division with **div_ceil**, the standard Rust method that rounds upward, and this one line is the single most reused formula in all of GPU programming.
2. The final match deliberately requests device 99, which no machine has, so we can watch a CUDA failure arrive as an ordinary Rust error value instead of a crash.

The rest of the file simply reads attributes through the same query mechanism the previous chapter introduced.

From the workspace root, after this, we will then run the planner:

```
cargo run -p grid_planner
```

Here, the reference machine reports its limits and lays out the candidate plans as below:

```
Context ready on NVIDIA GeForce RTX 3080.
Warp size: 32
Max threads per block: 1024
Max grid dimension x: 2147483647
Streaming multiprocessors: 68
1048576 elements -> 8192 blocks of 128 threads (120 blocks per SM)
1048576 elements -> 4096 blocks of 256 threads (60 blocks per SM)
1048576 elements -> 2048 blocks of 512 threads (30 blocks per SM)
1920x1080 image -> grid 120x68 of 16x16 blocks
Device 99 refused politely: InvalidDevice
```

If you could notice in the output, all the three shapes cover the same million elements, and all three are legal, since even 8192 blocks sit nowhere near the grid limit in the billions. The difference lies in how the work spreads across the 68 SMs, because smaller blocks produce more of them and give the hardware scheduler more flexibility.

The final line confirms the two-dimensional recipe. Our 1920 by 1080 image divides evenly into 120 by 68 blocks, so no overhang exists in either direction on this shape, though the guard pattern from a later chapter will still appear in image kernels because arbitrary sizes rarely divide so kindly. A grid of 8160 blocks also gives the scheduler plenty to distribute across 68 SMs, and that abundance, as we just learned from the warp model, is precisely what keeps the device busy.

Speaking CUDA in Rust Vocabulary

Errors become Results

Our planner just demonstrated the first translation. The CUDA C API reports failure through integer status codes that a C++ programmer must remember to check after every single call, and unchecked codes are a famous source of silent corruption. In Rust, every fallible call in **`cust`** and RustaCUDA returns a **`Result`**, so the compiler itself refuses to let us ignore a failure. The polite refusal we printed for device 99 was a **`CudaError`** value we caught with an ordinary **`match`**, no different from handling a missing file.

A second benefit appears in how errors compose. Because every CUDA failure is a value, our helper functions can bubble problems upward with the question mark operator, log them with useful surroundings, or convert them into domain errors the rest of the application understands. The same **`CudaError`** enum names each driver failure explicitly, from **`InvalidDevice`** to **`OutOfMemory`**, so a match arm can react to memory exhaustion differently from a bad argument. A C++ codebase builds such machinery by convention, while Rust hands it to us as language.

Cleanup becomes Drop

The second translation happened so quietly we could have missed it. Our program never released the context it created, yet nothing leaked, because the **`Context`** value freed its GPU state the moment it went out of scope at the end of **`main`**. This is RAII carried onto the device, and it will matter far more in the next chapter when device memory allocations follow the same rule.

The lifecycle appears in Fig 2.4 as a state diagram, and it applies unchanged to every GPU resource we will own in this book:

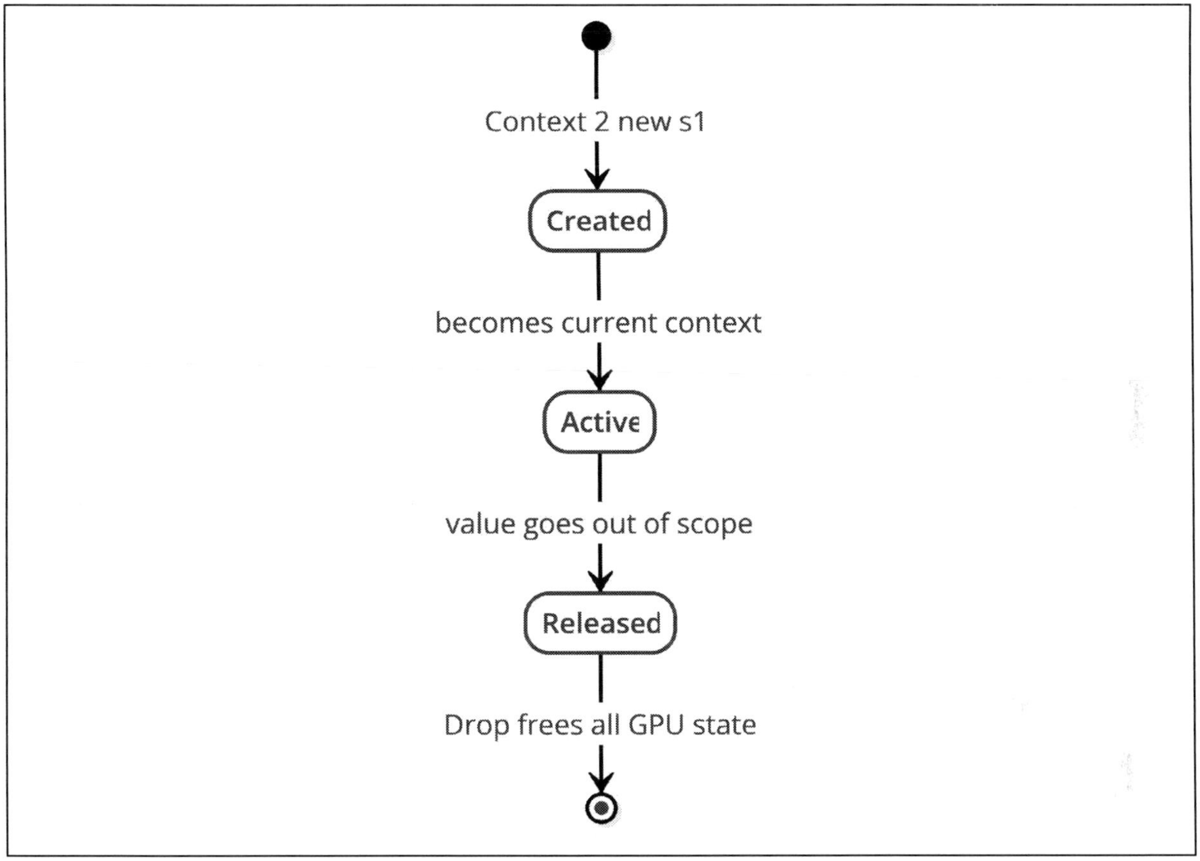

Fig 2.4: Life of GPU Resource

The same lifecycle will describe device buffers, modules, streams, and events in the chapters ahead, which is why we present it once and reference it forever. In each case, the constructor acquires GPU state, the value's scope defines its lifetime, and **`Drop`** performs the release in the correct dependency order without our involvement. The one habit this asks of us is to let scopes mirror our intent, so a buffer needed only for staging lives in a narrow block and returns its memory the moment the block ends.

Real Boundary of Unsafe

Every query, context, and plan so far lives in safe Rust, and the language guarantees hold completely with not one **unsafe** block across two chapters. The boundary arrives only when we launch a kernel, because at that moment Rust passes pointers to code the compiler never saw, and no static analysis can vouch for what happens on the other side. The real contribution of Rust is honesty about that line. In C++, the entire program sits past the boundary, while in Rust the boundary is a small, marked, reviewable region.

Our mental model is now in place. We can name the two worlds, the four organizational units, and the three levels of the thread hierarchy, and our **grid_planner** turns those names into numbers for the exact GPU on our desk. The **gpu_lab** workspace has gained its second member, and both members will keep serving us as diagnostic tools throughout the book.

In chapter 3, the model starts moving, because we will allocate real device memory, load a real PTX module, and command our first kernel launch from safe Rust.

CHAPTER 3
COMMANDING GPU

In this chapter, we will learn to start moving real data, starting with allocating the memory on the device, loading compiled kernel, launching it across thousands of threads, and reading the verified results back into a Rust vector. Our vehicle is RustaCUDA, the stable wrapper around the CUDA Driver API that we surveyed in the previous chapter, and every step happens from safe Rust except one deliberately marked launch. The kernel itself comes from CUDA C for now, because separating the host skill from the kernel skill keeps both learnable.

Along the way, we will meet the ownership types that make device memory feel like ordinary Rust, namely **DeviceBox** for single values and **DeviceBuffer** for arrays. We will dissect the **launch!** macro piece by piece, understand precisely why kernel launches sit behind **unsafe**, and practice the synchronization habit that every correct GPU program shares. Our **gpu_lab** workspace gains a third member named **vector_add_host**, and by the end it will add two million element vectors on the GPU and prove the result correct against a CPU check.

Initializing Driver API with RustaCUDA

Our new workspace member follows the pattern we established earlier, so we will only walk through the parts that differ. We will add a **vector_add_host** crate to **gpu_lab**, register it in the root manifest, and declare RustaCUDA in its own manifest. The crate compiles on the stable toolchain we already have, and it links against the CUDA driver at runtime rather than at build time.

So here, we will declare the dependency in **vector_add_host/Cargo.toml** as below:

```
[dependencies]
rustacuda = "0.1"
```

Three Startup Calls

We will pass three calls to move from a fresh process to a usable GPU. First, **rustacuda::init** loads the driver API, exactly as **cust::init** did in our earlier programs. Second, **Device::get_device** selects a GPU by index, which matters on multi card machines and stays harmless on single card ones. Third, **Context::create_and_push** creates a context on that device and pushes it onto a small stack of current contexts that the driver keeps per thread. The RustaCUDA documentation at **docs.rs/rustacuda** spells out this stack model, and we only need its simplest case.

The order of these three calls is fixed, and each one prepares the ground the next one stands on. If we skip initialization, the device query will have no driver to ask, and if we select no device, the context will have no hardware to bind to. Each call returns a Result, so a machine with no GPU or a broken driver announces itself at the first line of main with a readable error rather than a mysterious crash five calls later. This early, loud failure is exactly the behavior we want from infrastructure code.

Context Flags and Lifetime

The context call accepts flags that tune scheduling behavior, and the pairing of **`MAP_HOST`** with **`SCHED_AUTO`** is the documented default we will adopt without ceremony. For quick experiments, RustaCUDA also offers **`quick_init`**, a one-line shortcut that initializes the API and returns a ready context on device zero. We will use the explicit three call form in our project, because seeing each step once makes every later program readable, and we will happily reach for the shortcut in throwaway probes.

A context must exist before any allocation, module, or launch, and the driver enforces this rather than assuming it. If we request device memory without a current context, RustaCUDA returns an error value instead of crashing, which is the **`Result`** vocabulary from chapter 2 doing its job. For this reason, the context stays alive in a variable for the whole of **`main`**, and the underscore in its name only silences the unused variable warning rather than the ownership. The value still drops at the end and cleans up faithfully.

A small naming convention will serve us from here forward, and we may as well adopt it now. Our device buffers carry a **`d_`** prefix, such as **`d_a`** and **`d_c`**, while their host twins go without, so a glance at any line tells us which world its data lives in. The compiler would catch a confusion between the two anyway, thanks to the types, but our eyes read faster than our error lists, and a convention this cheap earns its keep in every listing for the rest of the book.

Moving Data with Ownership

In RustaCUDA, the device memory arrives as owned values rather than raw pointers, and two types cover our daily needs. A **`DeviceBox`** holds exactly one value on the GPU, which suits parameters and single results. A **`DeviceBuffer`** holds a contiguous array, which suits the vectors and images that our kernels chew through. We will see each type allocate in its constructor, copy with explicit methods, and free its memory in **`Drop`**, so a leak simply has nowhere to hide.

The two types and their everyday methods appear in the following Fig 3.1:

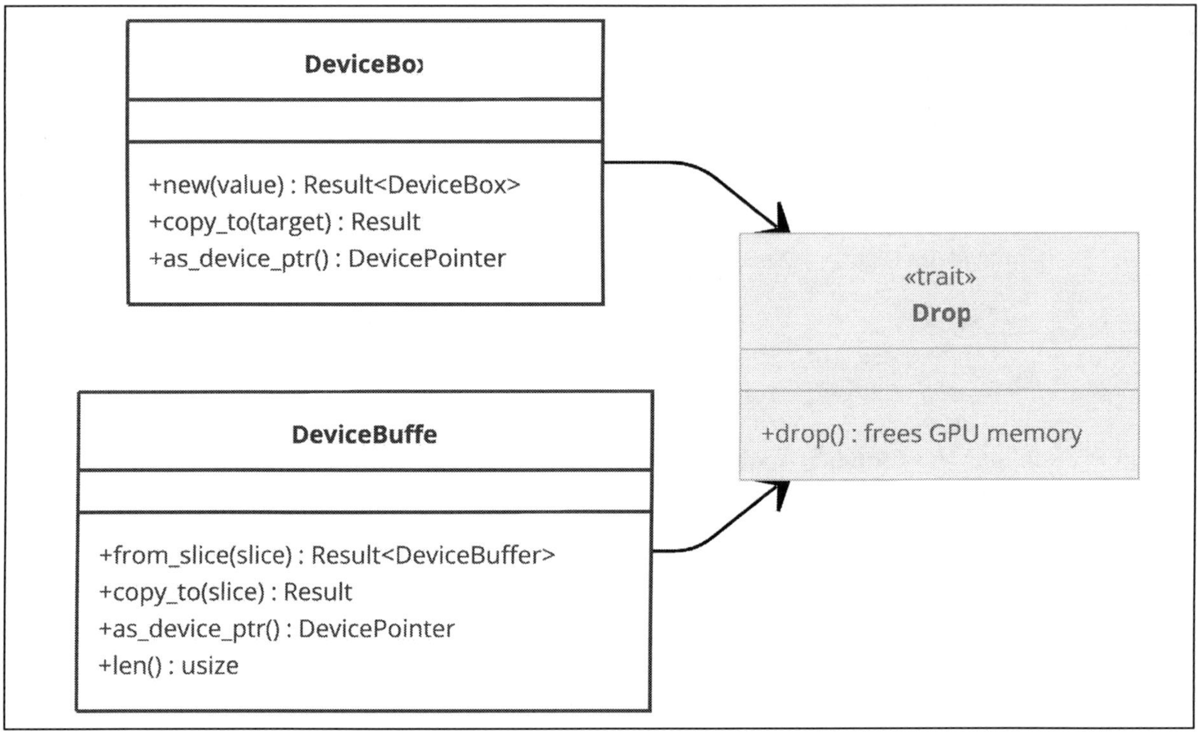

Fig 3.1: Ownership Types for Device Memory

Transfers with Direction

The transfer methods read like assignments with a direction. The **`from_slice`** constructor allocates device memory of the right size and copies the slice into it in one motion, while **`copy_to`** moves device contents back into a mutable slice we provide. The sizes must match exactly, and RustaCUDA checks this at runtime instead of corrupting memory the way a mistaken **`memcpy`** would. The symmetry with **`DeviceBox`** is complete, since it offers the same pair for single values. Every one of these calls returns a **`Result`**, in keeping with the vocabulary from chapter 2.

A three-line probe shows the same ownership pattern at its smallest:

```
let mut single = DeviceBox::new(&10.0f32)?;
let mut back = 0.0f32;
single.copy_to(&mut back)?;
```

Even this tiny exchange holds the full shape of GPU memory work. The constructor allocated four bytes on the device and copied our value across, the **`copy_to`** call brought it home into an ordinary stack variable, and the allocation will free itself when **`single`** leaves scope. Once this pattern feels boring, we have internalized it, and everything in the project below is this pattern repeated at a million elements. Such boring memory management is exactly the prize we came to

Rust to collect.

Bugs this Design Retires

We should pause on what this design quietly removed. In CUDA C++, the same work needs **cudaMalloc**, **cudaMemcpy** with a direction enum, and a matching **cudaFree** that someone must remember on every early return path. Each of those calls returns a status code that goes unchecked in an uncomfortable amount of real code. Our Rust version cannot forget the free, cannot mistake the direction, and cannot ignore the failure, and none of that safety required a single line of extra effort from us.

The retirement extends beyond leaks and directions into the quieter failure of mismatched sizes. Because a **DeviceBuffer** knows its own length, a copy into a slice of the wrong size becomes a checked error at the call site rather than a silent write past the end of an allocation. Anyone who has chased a corrupted result backward through a C++ codebase to a **memcpy** with a stale byte count will recognize the hours this single check returns to us. We trade nothing for it, since the length was always known.

Loading and Launching Kernels

Borrowed Kernel in CUDA C

A host needs something to launch, and this chapter borrows a kernel from CUDA C on purpose, because the separation lets us master the host side before the next chapter replaces the kernel language too. The canonical opener is vector addition, and NVIDIA ships an equivalent in its official cuda-samples repository at **github.com/NVIDIA/cuda-samples**. Each thread computes one global index from its block and thread identity, guards against overhang exactly as the previous chapter predicted, and adds one pair of elements.

We will now create **vector_add_host/kernels/vecadd.cu** with the following script:

```
extern "C" __global__ void vecadd(const float* a,
                                  const float* b,
                                  float* c,
                                  int n) {
    int i = blockIdx.x * blockDim.x + threadIdx.x;
    if (i < n) {
        c[i] = a[i] + b[i];
    }
}
```

Here, the **extern "C"** marker deserves a sentence, because without it the C++ compiler mangles the function name and our host would search the module for a symbol that no longer exists. With it, the module exports plain **vecadd**, which our launch macro will reference by name. The compilation to PTX takes one **nvcc** invocation with the **--ptx** flag, and we will park the result in a resources folder that the Rust build embeds.

So here, we will compile the kernel as below:

```
mkdir -p resources
nvcc --ptx kernels/vecadd.cu -o resources/vecadd.ptx
```

A quick word on failure modes will save future evenings. If **nvcc** is missing from the path, the shell reports command not found, and the fix is the **.bashrc** wiring from an earlier chapter. If the driver later rejects our PTX at load time with an invalid image error, the toolkit likely emitted PTX for a newer architecture than the driver understands, and a pinned target flag such as **-arch=compute_70** resolves the mismatch. We will find that both failures announce themselves clearly, and neither one corrupts anything.

From PTX File to Loaded Module

The loading of that PTX takes two short steps in Rust. The **include_str!** macro embeds the file into our binary at compile time, which spares us from shipping a loose file beside the executable, and **Module::load_from_string** hands the PTX to the driver, and the driver then compiles it for our exact GPU, the just in time translation the previous chapter explained. The **CString** conversion in between exists because the driver API expects C style strings. After this call, the module owns our kernel and can serve it by name.

A moment of appreciation belongs here, because this loose coupling is what makes the whole book possible. The module never asks which compiler produced its PTX, so today it accepts the output of **nvcc**, in chapter 4 it will accept PTX from the Rust compiler, and later it could accept the output of cuda-oxide, all through this identical pair of lines. Our host code therefore never changes as our kernel language does, and that stability is exactly the property previous chapter promised when it compared modules to shared libraries.

Dissecting launch Macro

The **launch!** macro is the heart of this chapter, and its syntax intentionally mirrors the triple chevron launch from CUDA C++. Between those chevrons, we will pass four values, namely the grid size, the block size, the bytes of shared memory to reserve, and the stream to queue on. Our shared memory stays at zero until later gives us a reason for it. After the chevrons come the kernel arguments, where buffers travel as raw device pointers through **as_device_ptr**, and plain numbers travel as themselves.

Now we reach the honest boundary that chapter 2 promised. The launch sits inside an **unsafe** block because Rust cannot verify anything about the PTX on the other side, neither the number of parameters, nor their types, nor how the kernel indexes our buffers. We are asserting to the compiler that the signature we call matches the signature we compiled, precisely the assertion a foreign function call makes. The RustaCUDA documentation frames launches in exactly these terms, and the framing tells us where our review attention belongs.

Synchronization Basics

Waiting for Stream

One more habit separates a working program from a lucky one. A kernel launch is asynchronous, so the **`launch!`** line returns immediately while the GPU works, and the host thread races ahead. If we read results without waiting, we receive stale or partial data, which is why **`stream.synchronize`** follows every launch in this chapter and blocks the host until the queued work completes. A homely picture keeps this straight. The stream is a ticket queue at a workshop, our launch drops a job ticket into it, and the synchronize call is us standing at the counter until the workshop confirms every ticket is done. The dropped ticket never implies the work has happened, and the confusion between those two moments is the single most common beginner defect in GPU code across every language. Once we feel the difference in our fingers, half of the strange bugs this field is known for simply never visit us.

The synchronize call also plays a second role that beginners rarely expect. Any errors from inside a kernel, such as an illegal memory access, do not surface at launch time, because the launch only queues work. They surface when the stream synchronizes, wrapped in the **`Result`** of that call. This is why our project checks the synchronize with the question mark rather than treating it as a formality, and it is also why a mysterious failure at a synchronize points backward toward the most recent kernel rather than at the waiting code itself.

Fixed Order of Host Program

The complete choreography now has a fixed order that we will reuse in every host program for the rest of the book. The initialization comes first, then the context, then the module and stream, then the buffers, then the launch, then the synchronization, and only then the copy back to host memory. Any reordering breaks something specific, and the misplaced synchronize is the classic offender, because such a program still compiles and often passes small tests before failing at scale.

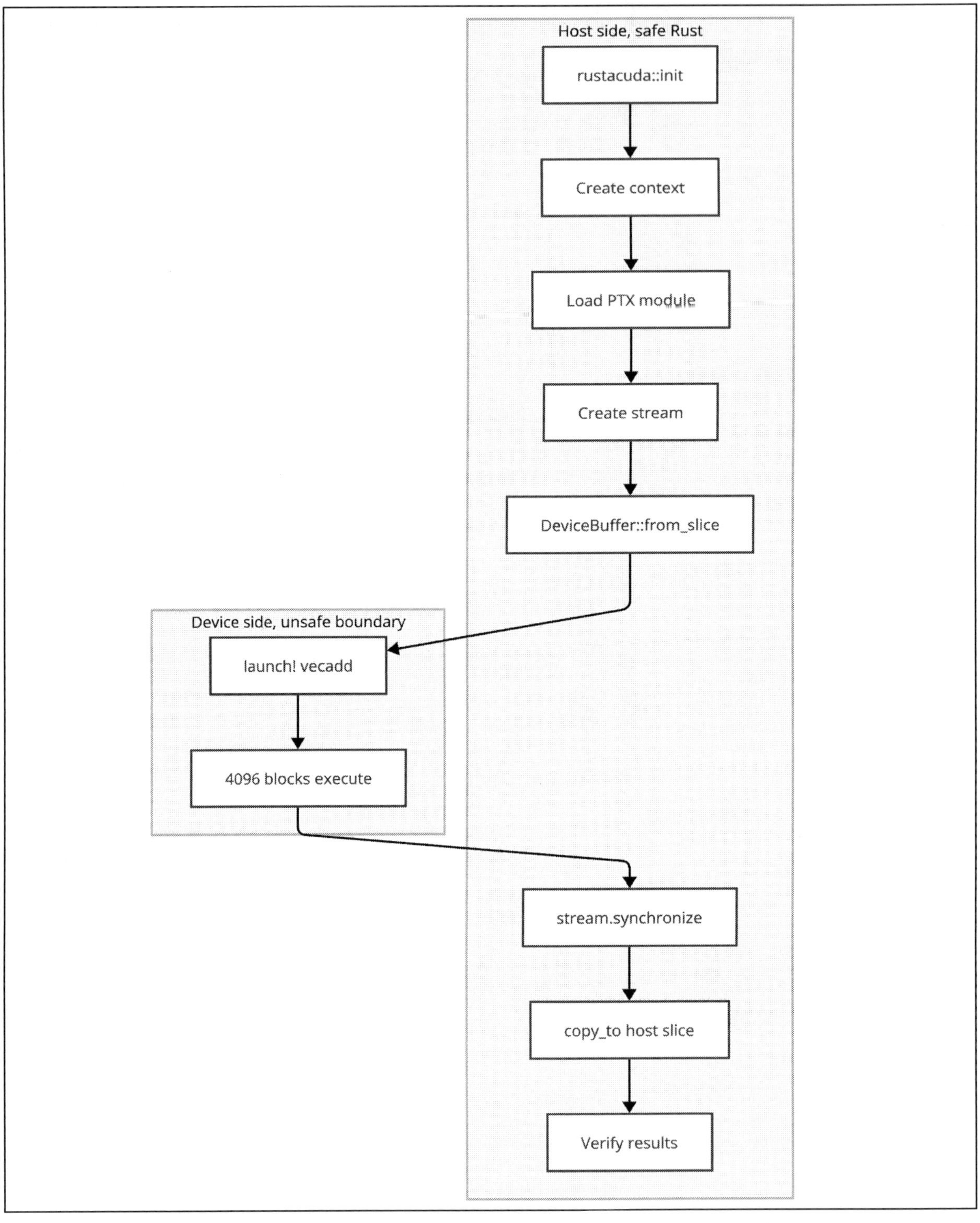

Fig 3.2: Host Program Pipeline

As shown above, the whole pipeline appears as a process flow, and the project that follows implements it line for line:

A printed copy of this figure beside the keyboard is less silly than it sounds, because the pipeline doubles as a debugging map. When a program misbehaves, we locate the first stage whose output we can verify, and the fault necessarily lives between there and the stage that disappointed us, which usually narrows an evening's suspects to two boxes.

Vector Addition with Prebuilt PTX Kernel

All these pieces will now assemble into our third workspace member. The program builds two input vectors of a million elements, one filled with ones and one holding each index, so every output element has a value we can predict without the GPU. It then walks the pipeline from Fig 3.2 and finishes with a full verification pass on the CPU. The argument list of the launch must match the CUDA C signature from vecadd.cu exactly, and we should keep that file in view while we read the launch.

Assembling Host Program

The listing below is longer than anything we have written so far, yet nothing in it is new, and that recognition is worth pausing on before we type. Every line either repeats a pattern from this chapter or reuses a habit from the previous two, so reading it should feel like revision rather than fresh material. Whenever a line does surprise us, the honest response is to revisit the section that introduced it, because the rest of the book assembles hosts exactly this way.

So here, we will fill **vector_add_host/src/main.rs** with the following:

```
use rustacuda::launch;
use rustacuda::prelude::*;
use std::error::Error;
use std::ffi::CString;

fn main() -> Result<(), Box<dyn Error>> {
    rustacuda::init(CudaFlags::empty())?;
    let device = Device::get_device(0)?;
    let _context =
        Context::create_and_push(ContextFlags::MAP_HOST |
ContextFlags::SCHED_AUTO, device)?;

    let ptx = CString::new(include_str!("../resources/vecadd.ptx"))?;
```

```
    let module = Module::load_from_string(&ptx)?;
    let stream = Stream::new(StreamFlags::NON_BLOCKING, None)?;

    let n: usize = 1_048_576;
    let host_a = vec![1.0f32; n];
    let host_b: Vec<f32> = (0..n).map(|i| i as f32).collect();

    let mut d_a = DeviceBuffer::from_slice(&host_a)?;
    let mut d_b = DeviceBuffer::from_slice(&host_b)?;
    let mut d_c = DeviceBuffer::from_slice(&vec![0.0f32; n])?;

    let block_size = 256u32;
    let grid_size = (n as u32).div_ceil(block_size);

    unsafe {
        launch!(module.vecadd<<<grid_size, block_size, 0, stream>>>(
            d_a.as_device_ptr(),
            d_b.as_device_ptr(),
            d_c.as_device_ptr(),
            n as i32
        ))?;
    }

    stream.synchronize()?;

    let mut host_c = vec![0.0f32; n];
    d_c.copy_to(&mut host_c)?;

    println!("Launched {} blocks of {} threads.", grid_size, block_size);
    println!("host_c[0] = {}", host_c[0]);
    println!("host_c[{}] = {}", n - 1, host_c[n - 1]);

    let all_match = host_c
```

```
        .iter()
        .enumerate()
        .all(|(i, value)| *value == 1.0 + i as f32);
    println!(
        "Verification: {}",
        if all_match { "every element matches" } else { "MISMATCH FOUND" }
    );

    Ok(())
}
```

A pair of choices in this file will reward a second look. The grid arithmetic reuses **div_ceil** from chapter 2, and with 1,048,576 elements and 256 wide blocks it produces exactly 4096 blocks, the very launch Fig 2.3 sketched. The verification closure recomputes every expected value on the CPU, and with inputs this predictable, each element must equal its index plus one. A million comparisons finish in milliseconds and give us certainty rather than a sampled impression, a habit worth keeping for every kernel we ever write.

Running and Reading Report

From the workspace root, we will now run the project:

```
cargo run -p vector_add_host
```

Our reference machine walks the pipeline and reports success:

```
Launched 4096 blocks of 256 threads.
host_c[0] = 1
host_c[1048575] = 1048576
Verification: every element matches
```

Here, a quiet detail in that report is worth savoring. The number 1048576 printed from the last element is our index 1048575 plus one, computed by thread 255 of block 4095, an ordinary thread among more than a million that ran. Not one line of the output distinguishes GPU arithmetic from CPU arithmetic, which is precisely the point. The exotic machinery of contexts, modules, and warps has collapsed into a program that reads like file handling code with one marked unsafe line at its center.

We should also temper any excitement about speed, because vector addition is a terrible benchmark and a wonderful teacher. The kernel performs one addition per element while we pay two full transfers across PCIe, so the copies dominate the arithmetic by a wide margin, and a plain

CPU loop would finish before our data even arrived on the device. Later, we measure this imbalance honestly, and later we give the GPU work worthy of its bandwidth. What matters today is that the pipeline is correct, repeatable, and entirely under Rust supervision.

Same Host in C++

Now, to weigh what Rust changed, we can hold our host against NVIDIA's own **`vectorAdd`** example from the cuda-samples repository at **github.com/NVIDIA/cuda-samples**, which performs the same addition through the runtime API. The C++ version dedicates roughly a third of its lines to checking status codes by hand, and every allocation must find its matching **`cudaFree`** along every path out of the function. Our version delegates all of that to **`Result`** and **`Drop`**, and the question mark operator turns each check into one character.

The comparison is not a rout, and honesty demands both columns. The C++ host compiles kernel and host together in one **`nvcc`** invocation, while we managed a separate PTX build step and an embedded resource. On its side, C++ also enjoys the runtime API conveniences, while the driver API asks us to manage a context explicitly. What Rust wins is the elimination of whole bug categories rather than keystrokes, and for a long-lived codebase that trade usually pays. Our numbers stay even, since both versions launch identical PTX at identical shapes. Our host skill is now complete for sequential work. We initialized the driver, owned device memory through types that clean up after themselves, dissected the launch macro, and confirmed a million results. Above all, we learned exactly where safe Rust ends and why, which turns the unsafe block from a warning into information. The **`gpu_lab`** workspace now holds three members, and the borrowed CUDA C kernel is the last foreign ingredient left in it.

CHAPTER 4
WRITING GPU KERNELS

In this chapter, the last foreign ingredient leaves our workspace. We will write GPU kernels in Rust itself, compile them to PTX with the Rust-CUDA backend we surveyed earlier, and launch them through a host that barely changes from chapter 3. The kernels stay deliberately routine, namely vector addition, SAXPY, and an image brightness pass, because the goal today is the toolchain rather than algorithmic novelty. As this chapter closes, the phrase written in Rust will describe both sides of our GPU programs truthfully.

We will let two new workspace members carry the work. A crate named **`kernels`** holds nothing but GPU functions marked with the **`#[kernel]`** attribute, and a crate named **`rust_kernels_host`** builds that PTX automatically inside its build script, embeds it, and launches each kernel with **`cust`**. We will also open the generated PTX file and read its header, because seeing our own Rust reduced to GPU assembly settles any doubt about what actually happened. A verification pass closes the loop for every kernel, exactly as chapter 3 taught.

How Rust becomes PTX?

From rustc to NVVM to PTX

The pipeline deserves a plain description before we ride it. The **`rustc_codegen_nvvm`** backend replaces the final stage of the Rust compiler, so our source still enjoys ordinary parsing, borrow checking, and optimization, and only the machine code emission changes. Instead of x86 instructions, the backend produces NVVM IR, a constrained dialect of LLVM IR that NVIDIA documents in its NVVM IR specification at docs.nvidia.com. The libnvvm library then turns that IR into the same PTX we compiled from CUDA C in chapter 3.

The practical consequence is wonderful and slightly anticlimactic. Our host pipeline from chapter 3 survives untouched, because the driver receives PTX and could not care less which language produced it. All that we learned about modules, streams, launches, and synchronization will transfer word for word, and only the producer of the PTX file changes. The arrangement also explains why later chapters can swap producers freely, since chapter 5 will slot a second compiler into the same position without disturbing anything downstream. We can trace both the build time and the run time halves in Fig 4.1 below:

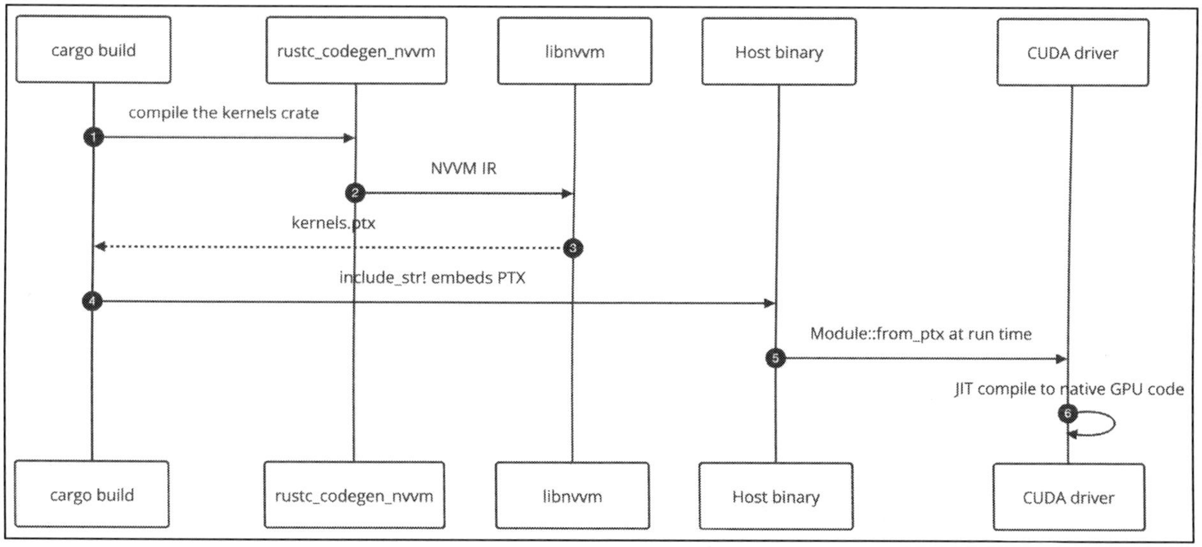

Fig 4.1: Rust Source to Running Kernel

Honoring Experimental Label

Ahead of any compilation, we must honor this project's experimental label from an earlier chapter. The codegen backend hooks into compiler internals, so it requires the exact nightly Rust release that the project pins in a **`rust-toolchain.toml`** file, and rustup switches to it automatically once that file sits in our workspace. The backend also builds against a specific LLVM, and the Getting Started section at **rust-gpu.github.io/rust-cuda** lists the packages for Ubuntu along with a ready-made container image. We will copy the pinned toolchain file from the project template unchanged.

A word of reassurance belongs beside that warning, because the pin is also what makes the setup reproducible. Once **`rust-toolchain.toml`** sits in the workspace, every machine that clones our project selects the identical compiler without any manual coordination, and a teammate cannot accidentally build the kernels with a nightly the backend never met. So the same file that marks this road as experimental also keeps everyone who travels it on the same pavement, which is as much stability as alpha software can honestly offer.

One Crate per Side

The layout question matters more here than in ordinary Rust projects, because kernel code and host code compile for different machines. The clean arrangement is one crate per side. Our **`kernels`** crate compiles to PTX and knows nothing about contexts or streams, while our **`rust_kernels_host`** crate compiles natively and knows nothing about thread indices. The split also pays at build time, since only the kernel crate needs the special toolchain treatment. The project documentation recommends exactly this arrangement, and the pieces connect inside **`gpu_lab`**.

The separation rewards us again whenever something goes wrong, because every failure now has an address. A compile error mentioning thread indices or intrinsics belongs to the **`kernels`** crate and the special backend, while a runtime error about contexts or launches belongs to the host crate and ordinary stable Rust. With the two worlds in one crate, those categories blur, and we end up rebuilding everything to test anything. With them apart, our debugging instincts from everyday Rust carry over unchanged.

'cuda_std' Toolbox

What Crate Provides?

Within the kernel crate, **`cuda_std`** will play the role that std plays everywhere else. Its thread module tells each thread who it is, with **`index_1d`** as the everyday call and richer two and three-dimensional variants beside it. Its math traits route floating point calls such as sin and sqrt to fast GPU intrinsics, and its assertion and printing macros give us familiar debugging reflexes on the device. The crate documentation at **docs.rs/cuda_std** catalogs the full surface, and we will meet more of it in later chapters.

The prelude deserves one practical remark before we lean on it. A single **`use cuda_std::prelude::*`** line at the top of the kernel crate brings the attribute, the thread module, and the math traits into scope together, so our kernel files stay free of import ceremony. This mirrors the role of the std prelude in ordinary Rust, and it means a kernel file can open with one line and get straight to work. We will follow that convention in every kernel listing from here to the end of the book.

What Device Side leaves Out?

Just as important is what the device side leaves out. The kernel code runs under **`no_std`**, so files, sockets, threads in the operating system sense, and most collections stay on the host where they belong. A kernel receives slices and numbers, computes, and writes results through pointers, and that austerity is a feature rather than a limitation. Every temptation the environment removes is a category of bug that cannot follow us onto ten thousand concurrent threads.

The absence that surprises newcomers most is heap allocation, because nothing in a kernel may call the global allocator. At first this feels confining, and then it reveals itself as a design compass. Any buffer a kernel needs must be allocated by the host and passed in, which forces every memory decision into the one place with a full view of sizes and lifetimes. Our kernels therefore read as pure functions over borrowed data, and that shape is precisely what makes them so amenable to testing and reasoning.

Kernel Writing Fundamentals

'kernel' Attribute and Unsafe

The **#[kernel]** attribute is the visible center of the system. It marks a function as a GPU entry point, arranges the calling convention the driver expects, and lets the backend check that the signature only uses types that can cross the boundary. We declare kernel functions **pub** so the PTX exports them by name, exactly the role **extern "C"** played in chapter 3. The attribute accepts configuration options as well, though none of them matter for the routine kernels of this chapter. Our functions also carry the **unsafe** keyword, and that honesty deserves its own paragraph.

A Rust kernel is unsafe for one precise reason. At run time, thousands of threads execute the same function over the same output pointer, and the compiler cannot prove that our indexing keeps their writes disjoint. The guard and the index arithmetic make disjointness true in practice, but the proof lives in our heads rather than in the type system. The Rust CUDA documentation states this openly, and in the next chapter we will see how cuda-oxide moves part of that proof into a library type. Until then, the **unsafe** marker keeps the obligation visible.

Cross Boundary Signatures

The signature conventions read naturally once we know the trick. The read only inputs arrive as ordinary slices such as **&[f32]**, and a slice is a fat pointer, so the launch will supply a pointer and a length as two separate arguments. The output travels as a raw ***mut f32**, written through pointer arithmetic after the bounds guard. That guard, **if i < a.len()**, is the same overhang protection an earlier chapter planned and the previous chapter wrote in CUDA C, now expressed with a method call on a slice we own.

A brief rule governs what may appear in a kernel signature at all. The arguments must be plain data, such as numbers, structures of numbers, slices, and raw pointers, because the launch copies them bit for bit to the device. An owned **String** or a **Vec** has no meaning across the boundary, and the backend rejects such signatures at compile time rather than at three in the morning. When a custom struct needs to cross, it derives a marker trait that confirms it is safe to copy, a pattern we will use later.

Host Side with cust

Build Script that Welds Two Worlds

A build script welds the two crates together, and this is the one truly new mechanism of the chapter. The **cuda_builder** crate, driven from the host's **build.rs**, invokes the special backend on our **kernels** crate every time we run **cargo build**, and it copies the resulting PTX into a resources folder. From there, the **include_str!** embeds it exactly as in chapter 3. One cargo command therefore rebuilds both worlds in the right order, and stale PTX becomes impossible rather than merely unlikely.

This quiet automation deserves a moment of gratitude from anyone who has maintained a hand-run **nvcc** step. In chapter 3, our PTX freshness depended on us remembering to recompile after every kernel edit, and human memory is precisely the component that fails on a busy afternoon. With the build script in place, the freshness guarantee moves from our discipline into the tool, which is the same trade Rust makes everywhere it can. We will never type a manual kernel compile again in this book.

Launching with Slice Expansion

The host code itself will feel like revision rather than novelty. We initialize with **quick_init**, the shortcut we met in chapter 3, load the module with **Module::from_ptx**, and fetch each kernel with **get_function**. The launch macro in **cust** matches the one in RustaCUDA almost symbol for symbol, with one convention to remember, namely that every slice parameter expands into its pointer and its length at the call site. The compiler cannot check this expansion, which is precisely why the launch remains unsafe.

A worked mnemonic keeps the convention from ever biting us. For a kernel signature that reads slice, slice, pointer, the call site must read pointer, length, pointer, length, pointer, in that exact order. Whenever a launch misbehaves inexplicably, our first check is to count arguments against this expansion, because a missing length shifts every later argument by one position and produces results that look corrupted rather than absent. One minute of counting routinely saves an evening of suspicion aimed at innocent kernel code.

We should also note what stays pleasantly identical, because familiarity is worth naming as much as novelty. The streams still order our work, the synchronize call still stands guard before every read back, and the **d_** naming convention from chapter 3 still tells us briefly where each buffer lives. A change of kernel language altered none of our host habits, which is precisely the stability the module abstraction promised us back earlier.

Everyday Kernels

Three Kernels in One Crate

We can now assemble the chapter's project. The **kernels** crate carries three functions that cover the everyday shapes of GPU work, namely element wise arithmetic over two inputs, the classic SAXPY update in place, and a saturating brightness pass over bytes. Each one fits in ten lines, and together they will exercise every convention this chapter introduced.

So here, we will create **kernels/src/lib.rs** with the following script:

```
#![cfg_attr(target_os = "cuda", no_std)]

use cuda_std::prelude::*;
```

```rust
#[kernel]
pub unsafe fn vecadd(a: &[f32], b: &[f32], c: *mut f32) {
    let i = thread::index_1d() as usize;
    if i < a.len() {
        let elem = &mut *c.add(i);
        *elem = a[i] + b[i];
    }
}

#[kernel]
pub unsafe fn saxpy(alpha: f32, x: &[f32], y: *mut f32) {
    let i = thread::index_1d() as usize;
    if i < x.len() {
        let elem = &mut *y.add(i);
        *elem = alpha * x[i] + *elem;
    }
}

#[kernel]
pub unsafe fn brighten(input: &[u8], gain: f32, output: *mut u8) {
    let i = thread::index_1d() as usize;
    if i < input.len() {
        let value = (input[i] as f32 * gain).min(255.0);
        *output.add(i) = value as u8;
    }
}
```

When we read the three functions together, we see how little ceremony a Rust kernel needs. Each one asks for its global index, guards against the overhang, and performs one line of arithmetic. The SAXPY kernel reads and writes through the same pointer, which is legal because each thread touches only its own element. The brightness kernel converts through **`f32`** to avoid integer overflow, clamps with **`min`**, and narrows back to a byte, a small pattern worth memorizing because image kernels reuse it constantly.

The first line of the file also rewards a glance, because the **cfg_attr** gate applies **no_std** only when the target is CUDA. This small conditional is what lets ordinary tools such as **cargo check** and our editor's analyzer read the crate as normal Rust, complete with autocompletion and inline errors, while the real GPU build strips the standard library away. We keep our familiar editing comfort on a crate whose true home is the device, and that comfort matters more than it sounds during a long kernel session.

A pair of short manifests will wire the build. The kernel crate declares **cuda_std** and builds as both rlib and cdylib, which lets the backend consume it while normal Rust tools still understand it. The host crate declares **cust** as a running dependency and **cuda_builder** as a build dependency, the compile time helper that will drive the PTX generation.

Once both crates are registered in the workspace manifest from an earlier chapter, we will then set up the two manifests as below:

```
# kernels/Cargo.toml
[dependencies]
cuda_std = "0.2"

[lib]
crate-type = ["cdylib", "rlib"]

# rust_kernels_host/Cargo.toml
[dependencies]
cust = "0.3"

[build-dependencies]
cuda_builder = "0.3"
```

Next, we will create **rust_kernels_host/build.rs** as below:

```
use cuda_builder::CudaBuilder;

fn main() {
    println!("cargo:rerun-if-changed=../kernels");
    CudaBuilder::new("../kernels")
        .copy_to("resources/kernels.ptx")
        .build()
```

```
        .unwrap();
}
```

Here, the rerun directive keeps cargo honest, because it re-triggers the kernel build whenever any file in the kernels crate changes. Absent that line, cargo would happily reuse yesterday's PTX after we edit a kernel, and we would chase a bug that no longer exists in the source. Every build system pain in GPU work has this flavor, and one printed line inoculates us against the worst of it. The **copy_to** destination lands inside the host crate, which keeps the embedded path in **include_str!** short and relative.

Running Three Launches

Our host program runs all three kernels in sequence over a million elements and verifies every result on the CPU, in the same spirit as chapter 3. The **vecadd** launch alone appears with full commentary, because the other two repeat the identical pattern with different arguments. We should watch the slice expansion convention at every call site, where each slice argument becomes a device pointer followed by a length.

For this, we will fill **rust_kernels_host/src/main.rs** with the following script:

```
use cust::prelude::*;
use std::error::Error;

static PTX: &str = include_str!("../resources/kernels.ptx");

fn main() -> Result<(), Box<dyn Error>> {
    let _context = cust::quick_init()?;
    let module = Module::from_ptx(PTX, &[])?;
    let stream = Stream::new(StreamFlags::NON_BLOCKING, None)?;

    let n: usize = 1_048_576;
    let block = 256u32;
    let grid = (n as u32).div_ceil(block);

    // vecadd: c = a + b
    let a = vec![1.0f32; n];
    let b: Vec<f32> = (0..n).map(|i| i as f32).collect();
    let d_a = DeviceBuffer::from_slice(&a)?;
```

```
let d_b = DeviceBuffer::from_slice(&b)?;
let mut d_c = DeviceBuffer::from_slice(&vec![0.0f32; n])?;

let vecadd = module.get_function("vecadd")?;
unsafe {
    launch!(vecadd<<<grid, block, 0, stream>>>(
        d_a.as_device_ptr(),
        d_a.len(),
        d_b.as_device_ptr(),
        d_b.len(),
        d_c.as_device_ptr()
    ))?;
}
stream.synchronize()?;

let mut c = vec![0.0f32; n];
d_c.copy_to(&mut c)?;
let ok = c.iter().enumerate().all(|(i, v)| *v == 1.0 + i as f32);
println!(
    "vecadd:   c[{}] = {} ({})",
    n - 1,
    c[n - 1],
    if ok { "verified" } else { "MISMATCH" }
);

// saxpy: y = 2.0 * x + y
let x: Vec<f32> = (0..n).map(|i| i as f32).collect();
let d_x = DeviceBuffer::from_slice(&x)?;
let mut d_y = DeviceBuffer::from_slice(&vec![1.0f32; n])?;

let saxpy = module.get_function("saxpy")?;
unsafe {
    launch!(saxpy<<<grid, block, 0, stream>>>(
```

```
            2.0f32,
            d_x.as_device_ptr(),
            d_x.len(),
            d_y.as_device_ptr()
        ))?;
    }
    stream.synchronize()?;

    let mut y = vec![0.0f32; n];
    d_y.copy_to(&mut y)?;
    let ok = y.iter().enumerate().all(|(i, v)| *v == 2.0 * i as f32 +
1.0);
    println!(
        "saxpy:    y[{}] = {} ({})",
        n - 1,
        y[n - 1],
        if ok { "verified" } else { "MISMATCH" }
    );

    // brighten: every 100 becomes 150 at gain 1.5
    let pixels = vec![100u8; n];
    let d_in = DeviceBuffer::from_slice(&pixels)?;
    let mut d_out = DeviceBuffer::from_slice(&vec![0u8; n])?;

    let brighten = module.get_function("brighten")?;
    unsafe {
        launch!(brighten<<<grid, block, 0, stream>>>(
            d_in.as_device_ptr(),
            d_in.len(),
            1.5f32,
            d_out.as_device_ptr()
        ))?;
    }
```

```
    stream.synchronize()?;

    let mut bright = vec![0u8; n];
    d_out.copy_to(&mut bright)?;
    let ok = bright.iter().all(|v| *v == 150);
    println!(
        "brighten: 100 -> {} ({})",
        bright[0],
        if ok { "verified" } else { "MISMATCH" }
    );

    Ok(())
}
```

The first build deserves patience, because cargo must compile the codegen backend itself before it can compile our kernels, and that one-time cost runs to several minutes on an average machine. Every later build reuses the cached backend and finishes in seconds, so the toolchain tax is real but paid once. If the build fails at this point, the toolchain pin from earlier in this chapter is the first thing to recheck, since a drifted nightly is the most common cause.

From the workspace root, we will now run the project:

```
cargo run -p rust_kernels_host
```

Our reference machine launches three Rust kernels and verifies all of them:

```
vecadd:   c[1048575] = 1048576 (verified)
saxpy:    y[1048575] = 2097151 (verified)
brighten: 100 -> 150 (verified)
```

All three verifications passing at once tells us something stronger than three lucky kernels. The entire chain held, from the nightly backend through NVVM IR, PTX generation, the build script, module loading, slice expansion, and finally a million threads per kernel. The SAXPY line deserves a second glance, since its last element prints 2097151, which is two times 1048575 plus one, computed in place by a kernel that read and wrote the same buffer safely. This habit of verifying correctness rather than assuming it is what lets the coming chapters build higher.

Inspecting Generated PTX

One inspection remains before we can claim the chapter's promise honestly. The PTX sitting in our resources folder is an ordinary readable file, and its header names the tools that made it, the architecture it targets, and the entry points it exports. To confirm those names takes one command, and a repeated check after every toolchain upgrade catch surprises early.

So here, we will look at the first lines of the artifact:

```
head -n 12 rust_kernels_host/resources/kernels.ptx
```

The opening lines identify the producer and our three exported kernels follow:

```
//


// Generated by NVIDIA NVVM Compiler


//
.version 7.1
.target sm_52
.address_size 64

.visible .entry vecadd(
```

The header reads like a birth certificate. The generator line names the NVVM compiler, the target line records the GPU architecture the PTX assumes, and each **.visible.entry** declaration matches one Rust function name from our kernels crate. No line of the file betrays its Rust origin, which is exactly the point of the whole pipeline. Any tool that consumes PTX, from our chapter 3 host to the profilers of a later chapter, accepts this file without knowing or caring where it came from. The file typically runs to a few hundred lines for our three kernels, and none of it needs hand editing in practice.

A slow scroll through the body pays a small dividend for the curious. Our bounds guard appears as a compare and branch near the top of each entry, the slice length travels as an ordinary parameter, and the arithmetic sits in a handful of fused instructions. None of this demand's fluency, and we will never write PTX by hand, but a passing familiarity turns the profiler listings of a later chapter from hieroglyphics into text we can skim with mild confidence.

Our workspace now computes with Rust on both sides of the PCIe bus. We wrote kernels with slices, guards, and one honest **unsafe**, taught cargo to build GPU code as a side effect of building the host, and verified three million results without touching CUDA C. The vecadd kernel from chapter 3 has been fully repatriated. In chapter 5, we will hand the same three kernels to cuda-oxide, NVIDIA's experimental compiler, and let the two toolchains compete for our affection with typed launches and bounds checked memory.

CHAPTER 5

CLEANER KERNELS WITH CUDA-OXIDE

In this chapter, we will meet the second compiler that turns Rust into GPU code, and we will let it compete directly with the toolchain from chapter 4. With cuda-oxide, NVIDIA's NVlabs team rebuilt the entire route from Rust source to PTX, and the result changes the daily experience in two visible ways. The kernels that fit the one thread one element pattern compile without any **`unsafe`** at all, and launches become ordinary typed method calls that the compiler checks like any other Rust function.

We will first understand how the machine works, because cuda-oxide rewards that understanding with fewer surprises. We will trace its compilation pipeline stage by stage, watch one build produce a host binary and a PTX file together, and learn the three tier safety model that decides where **`unsafe`** lives. Then, our three kernels from chapter 4 return, rebuilt inside a **`#[cuda_module]`**, and our workspace gains the member **`oxide_kernels`**. A closing comparison gives us a working rule for choosing between the two toolchains.

Second Compiler

Owning Full Pipeline

The philosophy of cuda-oxide fits in one sentence from its own documentation, namely use the best tool for each stage but own the full pipeline. The project runs the real rustc frontend on kernel code, so parsing, type inference, borrow checking, trait resolution, and monomorphization all happen exactly as they do for CPU code. The middle of the pipeline belongs to pliron, an IR framework written in pure Rust and inspired by MLIR, and the final step hands textual LLVM IR to the NVPTX backend that NVIDIA has refined inside LLVM for years.

The pipeline is worth seeing end to end, because every diagnostic we will ever meet names one of its stages. Our source enters rustc and leaves as Stable MIR, a versioned view of the compiler's mid level representation that survives nightly upgrades. The mir-importer crate translates that MIR into a pliron dialect, a lowering pass flattens it into LLVM dialect operations, an exporter prints an ordinary .ll file, and the external llc tool compiles that file to PTX. The architecture chapter at **nvlabs.github.io/cuda-oxide** documents each stage, and Fig 5.1 redraws it for our bookshelf:

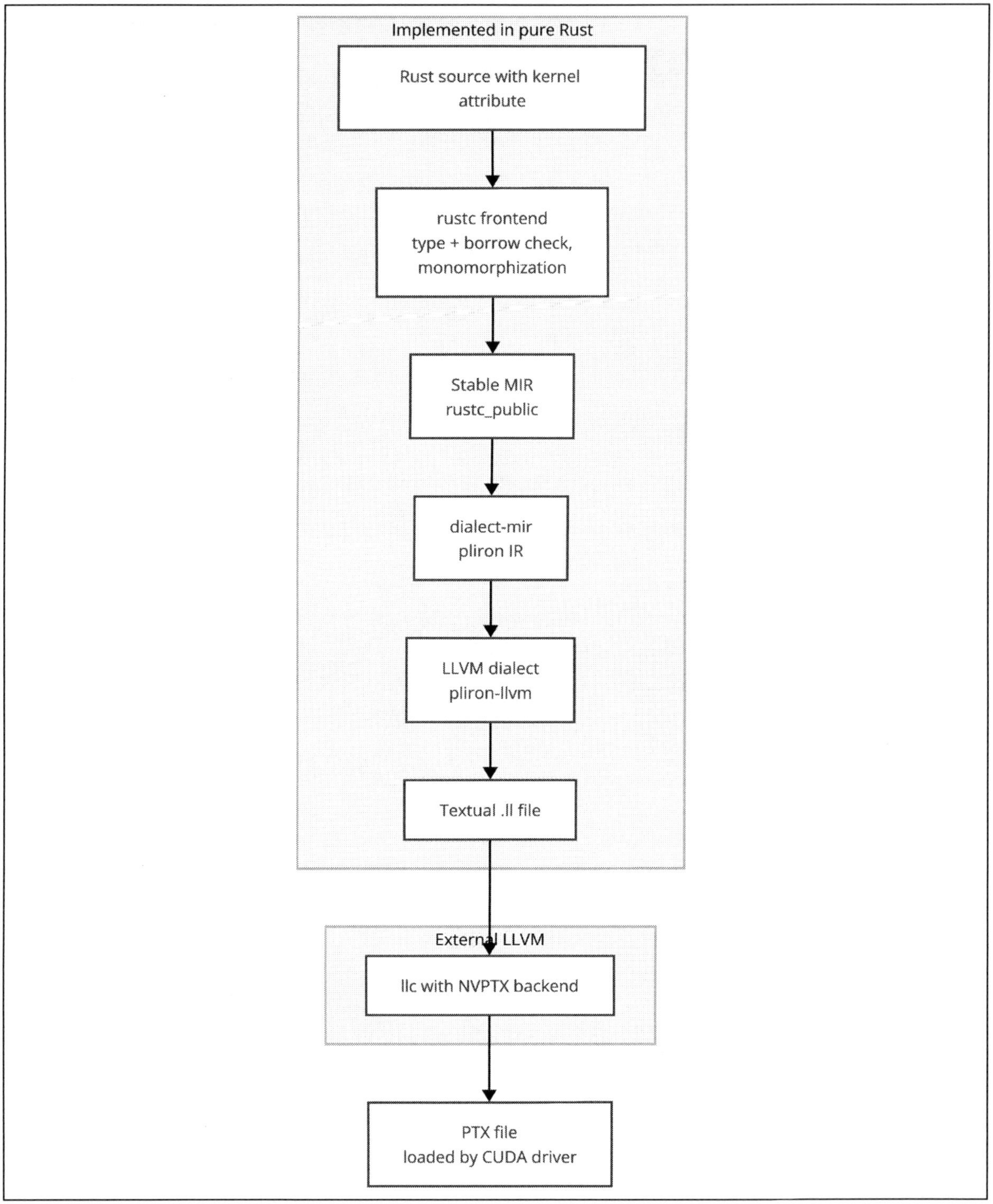

Fig 5.1: 'cuda-oxide' Compilation Pipeline

This choice of the real rustc brings gifts that a custom language could never afford. Every generic monomorphizes into concrete PTX kernels, match arms lower into optimized switches, dead code disappears before the GPU stages even start, and every error message arrives in the familiar rustc format with spans and suggestions. At no point does kernel code need a separate diagnostic dialect. Above all for this book, the borrow checker runs on device code unmodified, which is the foundation the safety model builds upon shortly.

One Build, Two Destinations

The user facing consequence is single source programming, and it removes the two-crate layout we maintained in chapter 4. Our host code and kernel code live in the same file, and one build compiles both. During code generation, the backend inspects every function and asks one question, namely whether the function is a kernel or reachable from one. The kernel side functions travel down the cuda-oxide pipeline into a PTX file, host side functions take the standard LLVM path, and a generic helper used by both compiles twice, once per target. The fork appears in Fig 5.2:

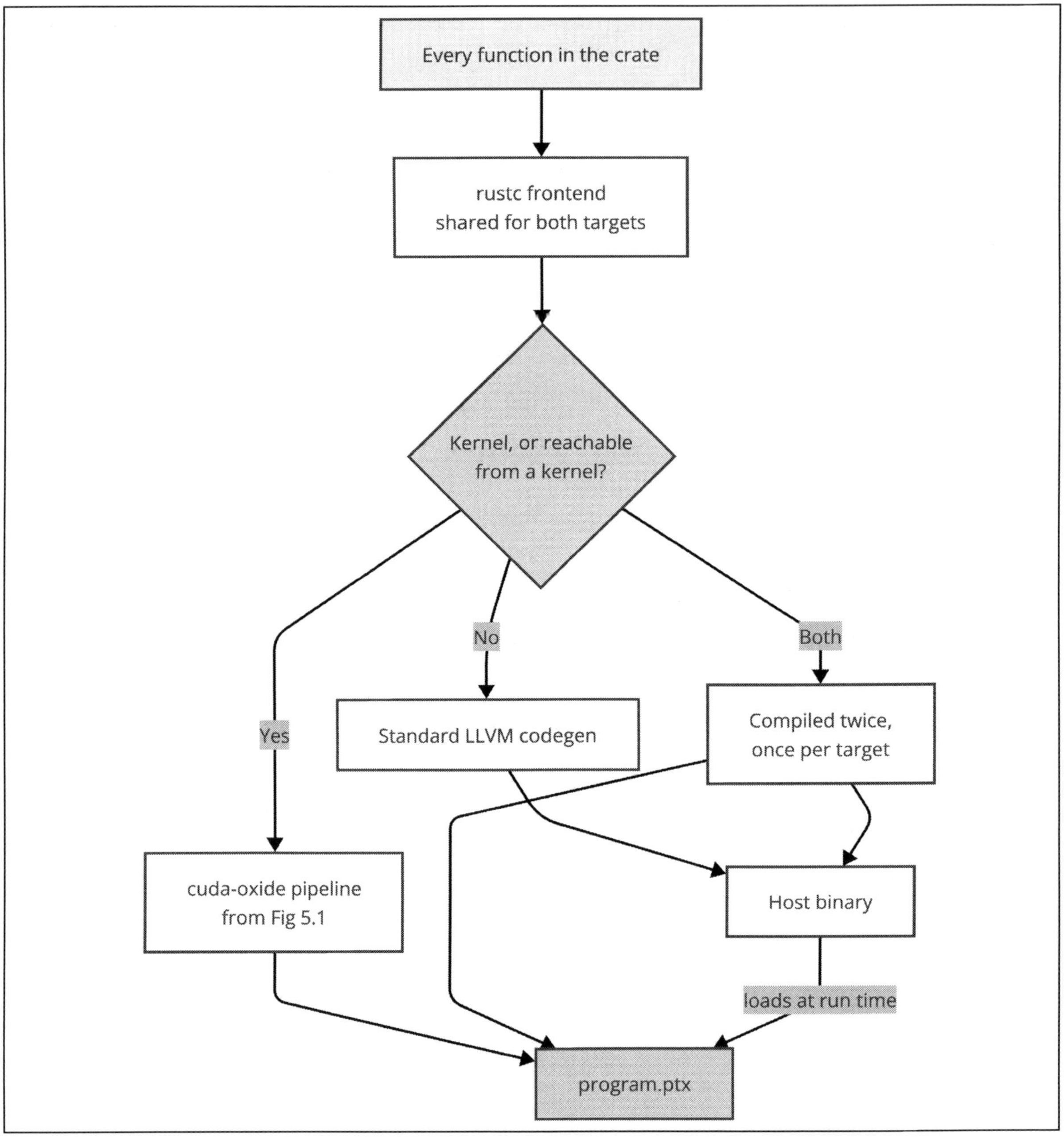

Fig 5.2: One Build, Two Destinations

One command therefore leaves two artifacts side by side in the target directory, the host binary and a PTX file named after our program. The binary loads that PTX through the driver at run time, exactly the mechanism Chapters 3 and 4 taught, and the **`#[cuda_module]`** attribute can even embed the PTX into the binary so nothing ships separately. Our hard-won mental model survives intact, and only the amount of ceremony around it shrinks. The arrangement will feel familiar to anyone who inspected the artifacts of chapter 4.

Installing Toolchain

The prerequisites are stricter than anything so far, and we will state them plainly before anyone loses an evening. The compiler targets Linux only and requires an Ampere or newer GPU, which means compute capability 8.0 and above, along with a recent driver, a CUDA Toolkit from the 12 series, and LLVM 21 or newer with the NVPTX backend for the final llc step. Our RTX 3080 from an earlier chapter reports compute capability 8.6, so it qualifies. The installation reference at **nvlabs.github.io/cuda-oxide** lists exact package commands for Ubuntu.

We will then run two commands to prepare the tooling. The cargo-oxide subcommand drives the whole build, and a built-in doctor validates every prerequisite in one pass, from the pinned nightly through libnvvm to the codegen backend itself. The pinned toolchain installs itself the first-time cargo runs inside the project, just as in chapter 4. We will find both commands finishing comfortably on a machine that already carries the setup from earlier.

So here, we will install the subcommand and let the doctor inspect our machine:

```
cargo install --git https://github.com/NVlabs/cuda-oxide.git cargo-oxide
cargo oxide doctor
```

If the doctor reports a missing llc or a clang header problem, the installation page maps each symptom to its one-line fix, and the repository also ships a ready devcontainer with the CUDA Toolkit, LLVM, and pinned nightly preinstalled for anyone who prefers a sealed environment. We should also repeat the honest label from an earlier chapter here.

Module and Kernel Macros

What Macros Generate?

We will let two macros carry the entire user experience. The **`#[kernel]`** attribute marks a GPU entry point, exactly as it did in chapter 4, and the **`#[cuda_module]`** attribute wraps a module of kernels and generates the host side plumbing we previously wrote by hand. That plumbing includes a typed load function that returns a module handle, plus one launch method per kernel whose parameters mirror the kernel signature. The launch method for our vecadd will literally accept two buffer references and one mutable buffer reference, in that order, or the program will not compile.

A useful way to picture the module attribute is as a code writer sitting beside us, producing the very plumbing we typed by hand across Chapters 3 and 4. The embedded PTX, the module load, the function lookup, and the argument marshaling all still exist, but they now come off the macro's pen instead of ours, generated fresh on every build from the kernel signatures themselves. Because the generator reads the same source we do, the plumbing can never drift out of date, which is the quiet failure hand written glue always risks.

What became Impossible?

We should pause to appreciate what just became impossible. In Chapters 3 and 4, the launch macro accepted whatever arguments we typed, and the match between call site and kernel signature was an assertion we made inside an **`unsafe`** block. With typed launches, an extra argument, a missing length, or a swapped buffer is a compile error with a helpful message, the same class of protection Rust gives any function call. The launch configuration also cleans up, since **`LaunchConfig::for_num_elems`** performs the ceiling division from an earlier chapter for us.

The mnemonic we practiced in chapter 4, counting pointers and lengths against the kernel signature, can now retire for cuda-oxide code, and its retirement is worth savoring. The whole class of shifted argument bugs, where one missing length turns every later parameter into quiet nonsense, no longer has a way to exist, because the generated launch method's signature is the kernel's signature. Our review attention, a finite resource, moves up from argument counting to algorithm reading, which is where it always belonged.

Safer Device Memory Access

The safety story is organized into three tiers, and the tier system tells us exactly where **`unsafe`** lives and why. The first tier covers kernels that the type system can prove race free, and they need no **`unsafe`** at all. The second tier covers cooperation through shared memory, warp intrinsics, and atomics, where **`unsafe`** appears in small scoped blocks with documented contracts, and a later chapter will live there. The third tier exposes raw architecture specific intrinsics for specialists building libraries. The model becomes a question we will ask about every kernel we write, and Fig 5.3 lays it out:

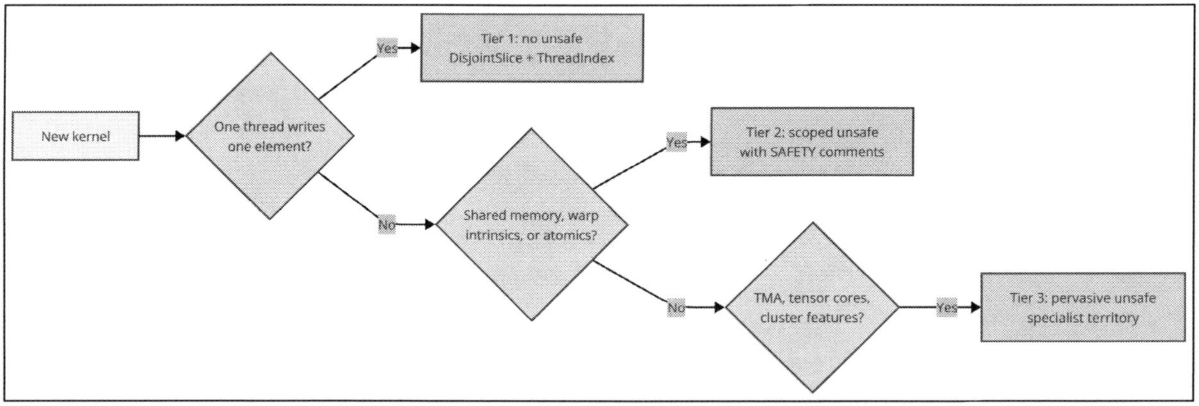

Fig 5.3: Need of Unsafe for Kernel

Witness Contract

The heart of the first tier is a pair of types that cooperate. A **`ThreadIndex`** is an opaque witness of a thread's identity, and it has no public constructor, so the only way to obtain one is through trusted functions such as **`index_1d`** that read the hardware registers. A **`DisjointSlice`** is a slice whose **`get_mut`** method accepts only such a witness and returns an **`Option`** that is **`None`** out of bounds. The hardware guarantees every thread a unique index, the wrapper guarantees bounds, and the borrow checker sees one mutable reference per thread. The contract appears in Fig 5.4:

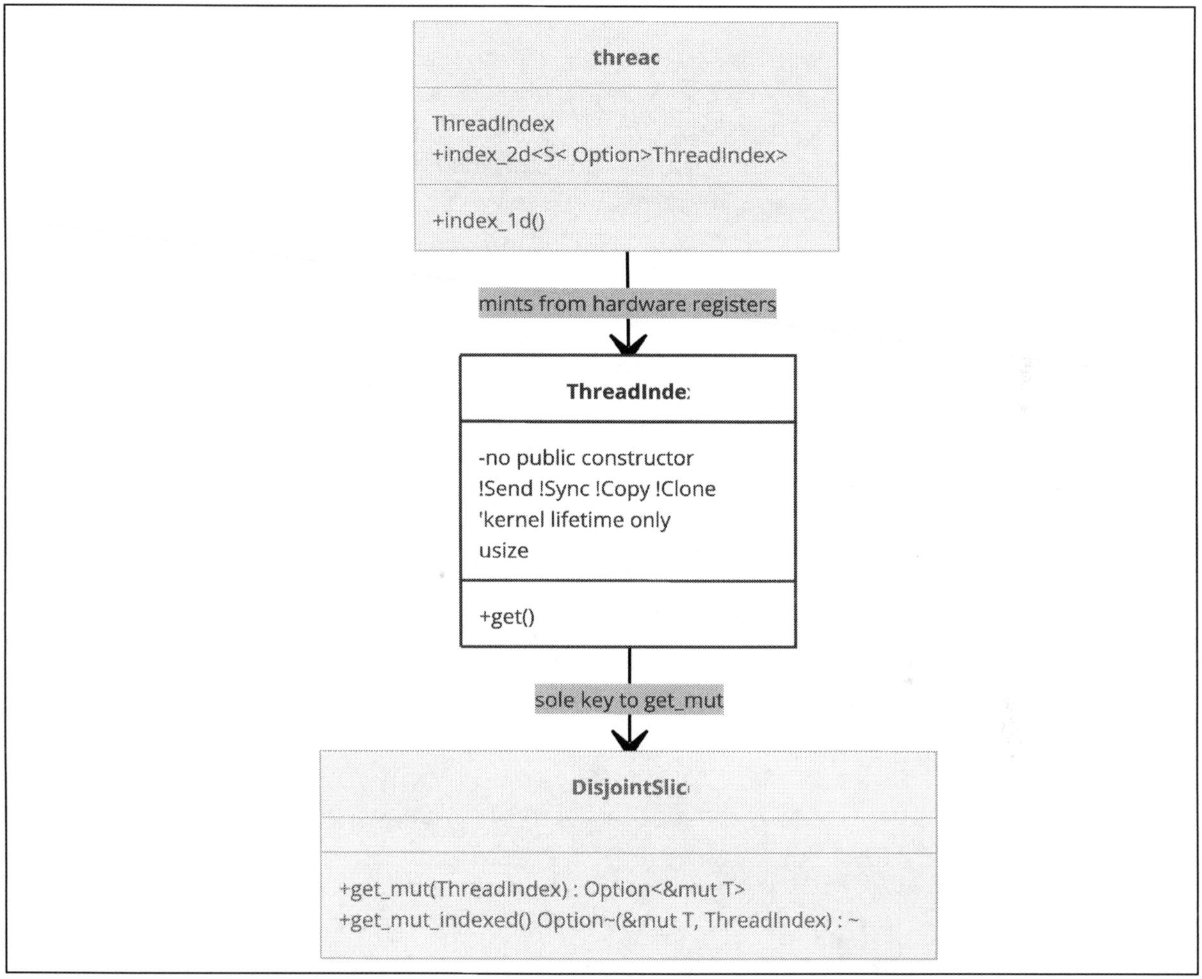

Fig 5.4: Witness Contract behind Safe Parallel Writes

The design closes the loopholes we might invent at two in the morning. A **`ThreadIndex`** cannot be copied, cloned, or sent, and a kernel scoped lifetime pins it to the stack, so one thread cannot stash its witness in shared memory for a neighbor to reuse. The two-dimensional variants will tie the stride into the type itself, and a mix of witnesses with different strides on one slice refuses to compile. The safety chapter of the cuda-oxide book walks through each of these guarantees with the reasoning behind them.

Honest Edges of Model

The same chapter is refreshingly honest about the edges, and we will inherit that honesty. For instance, warp level operations cannot verify thread convergence, so a wrong mask still hangs silently. Likewise, shared memory cooperation still requires manual discipline around barriers. A kernel parameter of type `&mut [T]` currently slips past the macro even though it aliases across threads, and the documentation tells us to treat any kernel that accepts one as entirely unsafe. The first tier is a real achievement, and it is not a force field.

This candor should raise our confidence in the model rather than lower it, because a safety system that names its own limits is one, we can plan around. We will treat the documented edges as fences we simply do not climb, so no kernel in this book accepts a `&mut [T]` parameter, and every barrier we write later follows the documented discipline exactly. A tool that overclaimed would deserve suspicion at every line, while this one has earned measured trust inside its stated boundaries.

Rust Features Inside Kernels

Generics that reach Device

Because the real rustc frontend compiles our kernels, language features work at a depth that surprises people arriving from CUDA C++. A kernel can be generic over its element type, and monomorphization stamps out one PTX kernel per concrete instantiation with no runtime cost. When something falls outside the supported subset, the compiler says so at build time in a normal Rust diagnostic, rather than through a mysterious launch failure at run time, and that difference alone repays the setup effort.

The practical payoff arrives the first time one algorithm must serve several numeric types. In CUDA C++, a kernel that adds **`f32`** today and **`f64`** tomorrow usually becomes a template with its own instantiation ceremony, while here it becomes an ordinary generic function with a trait bound, and each concrete use stamps its own entry point into the PTX. Our capstone later leans on exactly this convenience when its layers process both weights and activations through shared helpers.

Helpers and Closures on Device Terms

Beyond generics, the everyday conveniences of Rust carry over with pleasing fidelity. The helper functions marked `#[device]` factor shared logic exactly as ordinary functions do, so a clamp or an index calculation lives in one place and serves every kernel that needs it. Meanwhile, closures defined on the host can travel into kernels where the supported features list allows, which keeps small parameterizations readable without a proliferation of near identical kernels. Each of these features passes through the same frontend, so the borrow checker supervises all of it.

A sensible discipline keeps us clear of the alpha edges here as well. We will prefer named **`#[device]`** helpers over clever closure captures in every listing of this book, because named functions survive compiler upgrades more gracefully and read better in PTX dumps when a later chapter sends us hunting through generated code. The expressive ceiling of the toolchain is higher than our usage, and choosing the boring subset is exactly how one builds dependable work on adventurous foundations.

Kernels Rebuilt

One File from Both Worlds

Our project rebuilds the exact three kernels from chapter 4, which makes every difference between the toolchains visible line by line. We will create a new workspace member named **`oxide_kernels`**, and this time a single **`main.rs`** holds both worlds, the kernel module at the top and the host logic below it. The dependencies come from the cuda-oxide repository as git references, since the project versions its crates there during the alpha period.

So here, we will declare **oxide_kernels/Cargo.toml** as below:

```
[dependencies]
cuda-device = { git = "https://github.com/NVlabs/cuda-oxide.git" }
cuda-core = { git = "https://github.com/NVlabs/cuda-oxide.git" }
```

Each kernel takes its read only inputs as plain slices and its output as a **`DisjointSlice`**, and the **`get_mut_indexed`** call replaces the index and guard pair from chapter 4 in one motion. The bounds guard has not vanished, it has moved inside a library type where nobody can forget it. The saxpy output arrives as one mutable slice that each thread reads and writes at its own witness, the exact pattern the safety model was designed to bless.

First, a small orientation will help before we type, because a single file holding both worlds reads differently from anything in chapter 4. The **`#[cuda_module]`** block at the top is device territory, where DisjointSlice and witnesses rule, while everything below main is ordinary host Rust with buffers and streams. Our eyes will learn to switch registers at that module boundary the way they already switch at an unsafe brace, and the compiler enforces the distinction even when our attention lapses.

We will now fill **oxide_kernels/src/main.rs** with the following code:

```
use cuda_core::{CudaContext, DeviceBuffer, LaunchConfig};
use cuda_device::{cuda_module, kernel, DisjointSlice};
```

```rust
use std::error::Error;

#[cuda_module]
mod kernels {
    use super::*;

    #[kernel]
    fn vecadd(a: &[f32], b: &[f32], mut c: DisjointSlice<f32>) {
        if let Some((c_elem, idx)) = c.get_mut_indexed() {
            let i = idx.get();
            *c_elem = a[i] + b[i];
        }
    }

    #[kernel]
    fn saxpy(alpha: f32, x: &[f32], mut y: DisjointSlice<f32>) {
        if let Some((y_elem, idx)) = y.get_mut_indexed() {
            *y_elem = alpha * x[idx.get()] + *y_elem;
        }
    }

    #[kernel]
    fn brighten(input: &[u8], gain: f32, mut output: DisjointSlice<u8>) {
        if let Some((out_elem, idx)) = output.get_mut_indexed() {
            let value = (input[idx.get()] as f32 * gain).min(255.0);
            *out_elem = value as u8;
        }
    }
}

fn main() -> Result<(), Box<dyn Error>> {
    let ctx = CudaContext::new(0)?;
    let stream = ctx.default_stream();
```

```
    let module = kernels::load(&ctx)?;

    let n: usize = 1_048_576;
    let cfg = LaunchConfig::for_num_elems(n as u32);

    // vecadd: c = a + b
    let host_a = vec![1.0f32; n];
    let host_b: Vec<f32> = (0..n).map(|i| i as f32).collect();
    let a = DeviceBuffer::from_host(&stream, &host_a)?;
    let b = DeviceBuffer::from_host(&stream, &host_b)?;
    let mut c = DeviceBuffer::<f32>::zeroed(&stream, n)?;

    module.vecadd(&stream, cfg, &a, &b, &mut c)?;
    let out = c.to_host_vec(&stream)?;
    let ok = out.iter().enumerate().all(|(i, v)| *v == 1.0 + i as f32);
    println!(
        "vecadd:   c[{}] = {} ({})",
        n - 1,
        out[n - 1],
        if ok { "verified" } else { "MISMATCH" }
    );

    // saxpy: y = 2.0 * x + y
    let host_x: Vec<f32> = (0..n).map(|i| i as f32).collect();
    let x = DeviceBuffer::from_host(&stream, &host_x)?;
    let mut y = DeviceBuffer::from_host(&stream, &vec![1.0f32; n])?;

    module.saxpy(&stream, cfg, 2.0f32, &x, &mut y)?;
    let out = y.to_host_vec(&stream)?;
    let ok = out.iter().enumerate().all(|(i, v)| *v == 2.0 * i as f32 +
1.0);
    println!(
        "saxpy:    y[{}] = {} ({})",
```

```
        n - 1,
        out[n - 1],
        if ok { "verified" } else { "MISMATCH" }
    );

    // brighten: every 100 becomes 150 at gain 1.5
    let pixels = vec![100u8; n];
    let input = DeviceBuffer::from_host(&stream, &pixels)?;
    let mut output = DeviceBuffer::<u8>::zeroed(&stream, n)?;

    module.brighten(&stream, cfg, &input, 1.5f32, &mut output)?;
    let out = output.to_host_vec(&stream)?;
    let ok = out.iter().all(|v| *v == 150);
    println!(
        "brighten: 100 -> {} ({})",
        out[0],
        if ok { "verified" } else { "MISMATCH" }
    );

    Ok(())
}
```

Reading Rebuilt Kernels

When we set vecadd beside its chapter 4 twin, the comparison repays the whole chapter. The old version computed an index, guarded it manually, and dereferenced a raw pointer inside **`unsafe`**, while the new version asks the output slice for this thread's element and receives either a checked mutable reference or **`None`**. The saxpy kernel shows the same shape with a read of the old value through the same reference. Not one **`unsafe`** block appears in the file, and the borrow checker accepted every line on its ordinary terms.

The host half shrinks just as visibly. The generated **`kernels::load`** function returns a handle whose methods are our kernels, so the stringly typed **`get_function`** lookup from chapter 4 disappears, and with it the possibility of a typo that only fails at run time. The buffers move with **`DeviceBuffer::from_host`** and **`to_host_vec`**, both tied to a stream, and **`LaunchConfig::for_num_elems`** computes our grid shape. Every call still returns a **`Result`**, so the error vocabulary from an earlier chapter continues unchanged. The whole host says strictly more to the compiler in roughly half the lines of chapter 4.

Running through cargo oxide

From the crate directory, we will now build and run through the subcommand:

```
cargo oxide run
```

Our reference machine compiles both halves and verifies all three kernels:

```
vecadd:   c[1048575] = 1048576 (verified)
saxpy:    y[1048575] = 2097151 (verified)
brighten: 100 -> 150 (verified)
```

A glance at the target directory completes the picture, because beside the host binary sits the PTX file that the pipeline from Fig 5.1 produced, and nothing stops us from opening it exactly as we did in chapter 4. The same three entry points appear under their hashed cuda-oxide names. Under the surface, everything we learned in the first four chapters still happens, and the entire difference is how much of it the compiler now supervises for us.

One habit is worth adopting while the subcommand is fresh, namely running **`cargo oxide doctor`** again after any driver, toolkit, or LLVM upgrade. Because the pipeline leans on an external **`llc`** and a pinned nightly, a system update can quietly shift a prerequisite out from under us, and the doctor catches the drift in seconds where a failed build would spend our patience in minutes. This is the same early loud failure principle we praised earlier, applied to the toolchain itself rather than to the program.

Choosing Toolchain per Task

With both compilers in hand, a working decision rule falls out of our experience. We reach for cuda-oxide when the kernels fit the first two tiers, when typed launches would prevent real mistakes, and when Ampere or newer hardware is guaranteed, and we accept its alpha volatility in exchange. We reach for Rust-CUDA when older GPUs must run our PTX or when we prefer its more settled crate surface, and we keep RustaCUDA for hosts that launch PTX from any origin. No rule forces one loyalty, and our workspace now demonstrates all three coexisting peacefully.

The rule has one more clause worth writing down, namely that mixing is normal rather than shameful. A production system might keep its stable, performance proven kernels on the chapter 4 toolchain while prototyping new ones under cuda-oxide for the typed launches, and the shared PTX contract means the two families can even load into one host program. In young ecosystems, toolchain choices are rentals rather than marriages, and our workspace layout keeps every lease easy to end.

Our three kernels now exist in two Rust dialects of GPU programming, and the comparison taught us more than either version alone. We watched a compiler move race freedom from a comment into the type system, felt typed launches remove a whole category of launch time surprises, and confirmed the results down to the last element. The workspace holds six members across three toolchains. In chapter 6, we will stop admiring kernels and start feeding them properly, because memory movement, not arithmetic, decides GPU performance, and our transfers so far have been naive.

Chapter 6
Mastering GPU Memory

In this chapter, we will learn the single most valuable skill in GPU programming, which is feeding data to the processor properly. Our kernels so far computed almost nothing, yet even they spent most of their lives waiting on memory, and every real workload we build from here will live or die by its access patterns. We will walk the device memory hierarchy from registers to global memory, learn why some host memory transfers twice as fast, and meet the coalescing rules that decide whether thirty two threads make one memory transaction or thirty two.

Our project turns the theory into numbers. We will optimize a matrix transpose in three visible steps, from a naive kernel to a shared memory tiled version with a bank conflict fix, and we will measure effective bandwidth after every step against the ceiling set by a plain copy kernel. The **`kernels`** crate from an earlier chapter gains the new GPU functions, a new member named **`memory_lab`** runs the measurements, and the bandwidth table at the end becomes our first honest performance result in this book.

Memory Hierarchy Deciding Performance

Map of Five Memories

A GPU offers several memories with wildly different personalities, and the CUDA Best Practices material at docs.nvidia.com opens its performance advice with exactly this map. The registers are the fastest and belong to single threads. The shared memory tier sits on each SM, serves whole thread blocks at latencies close to registers, and holds tens of kilobytes. The constant memory broadcasts small read only values efficiently to many threads at once. The global memory is the gigabytes we allocate from the host, and it is both the largest and the slowest layer by two orders of magnitude.

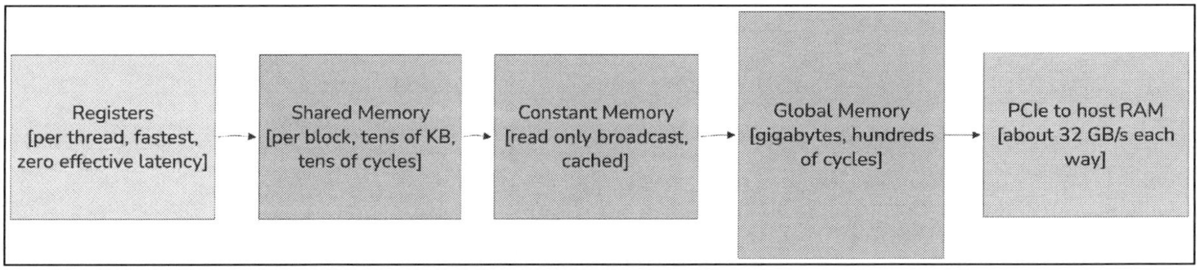

Fig 6.1: Device Memory Hierarchy

The numbers behind the map explain most GPU performance stories. A register access costs effectively nothing, shared memory responds in tens of cycles, and global memory keeps a warp waiting for hundreds. Earlier, we saw how the hardware hides that wait when enough warps are resident, but a hidden wait creates no extra bandwidth. Our RTX 3080 moves at most 760 gigabytes per second from global memory, and every kernel we ever write shares that ceiling. The craft of this chapter is spending those gigabytes wisely.

A homely picture holds the whole map together. The registers are the tools in a worker's hands, the shared memory is the workbench a small team gathers around, and the global memory is the warehouse across the yard, enormous and slow to visit. Every optimization in this chapter amounts to fewer warehouse trips per useful result, either by walking the aisles in order or by carrying full boxes to the workbench before unpacking them. Once we hold that picture, the vocabulary of tiles, strides, and banks stops feeling exotic.

Reading Map from Code

Every buffer we have created since an earlier chapter, lives in global memory, and the registers have been managed invisibly by the compilers. The shared memory appeared only as the zero we passed inside launch chevrons. That accounting changes today for shared memory and stays automatic for registers, which the backends allocate per thread from each SM register file. The constant memory earns a brief appearance later, where library parameters suit it well. The hierarchy is small enough to memorize, and the memorizing pays off daily.

One more resident of the hierarchy deserves a warning label. When a kernel needs more registers than the SM can grant, the compiler spills the excess into local memory, a private slice of global memory with a deceptively cozy name. A spilled variable therefore pays global latency on every access, and heavy spilling can quietly erase a clever optimization. We cannot see spills in source code, but a later chapter reads them directly from compiler reports, and until then modest kernels like ours stay comfortably within their register budgets.

Host Memory Transfers Faster

Pageable vs. Pinned

The transfer speeds from an earlier chapter hid one variable, namely how the host side memory was allocated. An ordinary Rust **`Vec`** lives in pageable memory, which the operating system may move or swap, so the driver must first copy it into an internal staging area before the GPU can pull it across PCIe. The pinned variety, also called page locked memory, is promised to stay put, and the GPU reads it directly with no staging hop. The CUDA Best Practices documentation reports substantially higher throughput for pinned transfers, and we can verify that claim in minutes.

The staging hop explains the entire difference, so it deserves one careful sentence. With pageable memory, every transfer becomes two copies, one from our **`Vec`** into the driver's locked staging buffer and one from that buffer across the bus, and the first copy runs at ordinary system memory speed on a busy CPU. With pinned memory, the second copy is the only copy. So, the speedup we are about to measure is not the bus getting faster, it is half the work disappearing.

Measuring Difference

In **`cust`**, pinned memory arrives as **`LockedBuffer`**, an owned type that allocates page locked storage and frees it in **Drop**, the same ownership contract our device buffers follow. Our probe copies a quarter gigabyte to the device ten times from a **Vec** and then ten times from a **LockedBuffer**, and it times both runs with **Instant**. The new member **memory_lab** follows the setup pattern from an earlier chapter, with **cust** as its only dependency.

So here, we will open **memory_lab/src/main.rs** with the transfer probe as below:

```
use cust::memory::LockedBuffer;
use cust::prelude::*;
use std::time::Instant;

fn gbs(bytes: usize, iters: u32, secs: f64) -> f64 {
    (bytes as f64 * iters as f64) / secs / 1e9
}

fn transfer_probe() -> Result<(), Box<dyn std::error::Error>> {
    let n: usize = 64 * 1024 * 1024; // 256 MB of f32
    let bytes = n * 4;

    let pageable = vec![1.0f32; n];
    let mut device = DeviceBuffer::from_slice(&pageable)?;

    let start = Instant::now();
    for _ in 0..10 {
        device.copy_from(&pageable)?;
    }
    println!("pageable: {:>5.1} GB/s", gbs(bytes, 10,
start.elapsed().as_secs_f64()));

    let pinned = LockedBuffer::new(&1.0f32, n)?;
    let start = Instant::now();
    for _ in 0..10 {
        device.copy_from(pinned.as_slice())?;
    }
    println!("pinned:   {:>5.1} GB/s", gbs(bytes, 10,
start.elapsed().as_secs_f64()));
```

```
    Ok(())
}
```

The probe reports both speeds side by side on our reference machine:

```
pageable:   11.9 GB/s
pinned:     24.3 GB/s
```

Our reference machine reports the gap plainly, with pageable transfers reaching roughly twelve gigabytes per second and pinned transfers roughly twenty-four, close to the practical limit of a PCIe 4.0 x16 link. The doubling is free in code terms, since the two calls differ by one type name. The pinned option is not a default, however, because the operating system cannot swap it, and pinning many gigabytes can starve the rest of the machine. The working rule is to pin the buffers that participate in repeated or overlapped transfers, which is exactly the scenario we meet later.

The probe also models a measurement habit we will keep for the rest of the book. We timed ten iterations rather than one, so a scheduler hiccup or a background process cannot masquerade as a result, and we computed bandwidth from total bytes and total seconds rather than trusting any single stopwatch reading. Whenever a performance claim appears in these chapters, this same shape of loop stands behind it, and we would encourage the identical skepticism toward any number measured only once.

Essential Access Patterns

Coalescing across Warp

The coalescing rule turns thirty-two memory requests into one. When the threads of a warp read consecutive addresses, the hardware merges those reads into a small number of wide transactions, and the warp enjoys the full bandwidth of the bus. When threads read addresses separated by a stride, the same instruction shatters into many transactions, and effective bandwidth divides accordingly. In How to Access Global Memory Efficiently on the NVIDIA technical blog, Harris explains the mechanics, and the two patterns sit side by side in Fig 6.2:

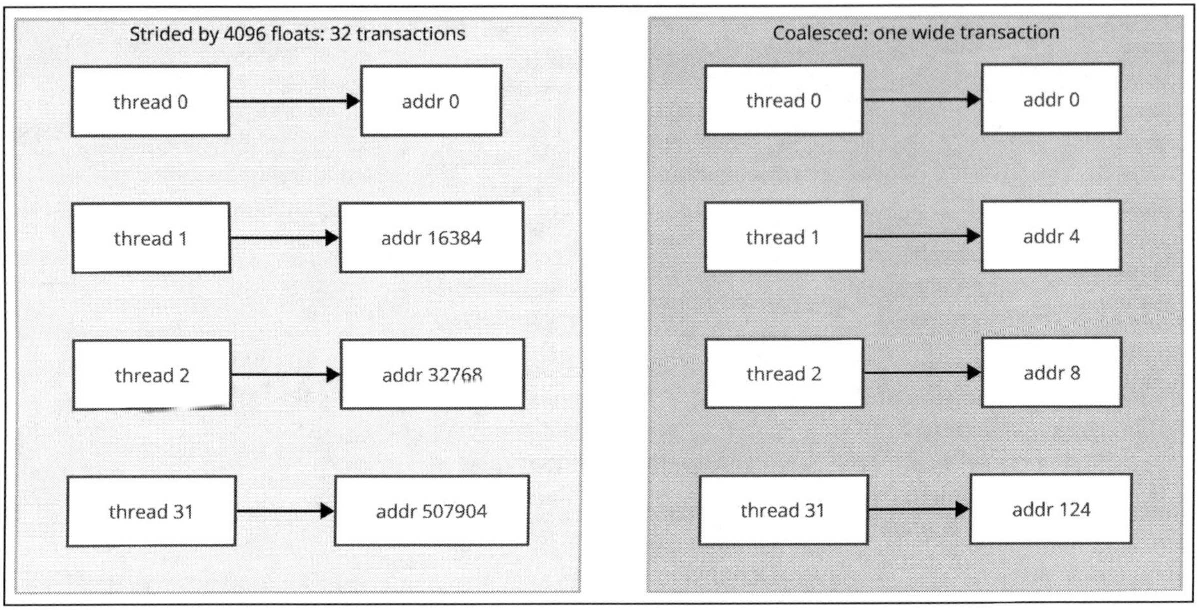

Fig 6.2: Coalesced vs. Strided Access across One Warp

The pattern hides in our index arithmetic rather than in any special syntax. The expression input[y * width + x], with x derived from the fast moving thread index, walks consecutive addresses across a warp and coalesces perfectly. The expression input[x * width + y] under the same indices jumps a full row between neighboring threads and shatters. No syntax in Rust or CUDA C marks the second as slow, which is why transposes, and any kernel that changes data layout, are where beginners meet the problem first.

Detecting Strides and Choosing Layouts

Happily, detection is easier than memorization. Whenever a kernel subscript multiplies the fast thread index by anything larger than one, we should suspect a strided access and expect the profiler of a later chapter to confirm it. Until we own that profiler skill, measured bandwidth is our detector, and the transpose project below shows the signature clearly, since the same arithmetic with swapped subscripts loses most of its throughput. A kernel that reads well and writes badly, or the reverse, lands exactly in the middle of the two extremes.

A related habit concerns the shape of our records. An array of structures scatters each field across memory, so a warp reading one field from thirty-two records strides by the structure size and shatters. A structure of arrays keeps each field contiguous, and the same read coalesces. In Rust, the second layout stays pleasant to build with ordinary vectors per field, and the pipeline of a later chapter adopts it deliberately. When a kernel processes only some fields of a record, the layout choice alone can double throughput.

None of these habits require heroics, and that is the encouraging note to end the section on. We are not rewriting algorithms or learning assembly, we are choosing which subscript multiplies what, which field lives beside which, and which buffer earns pinning. Each choice is a line or two at design time and nearly free to get right from the start, while each is expensive to retrofit after a codebase has calcified around the wrong layout. The checklist is short, and the transpose below shows the largest of these effects with numbers attached.

Ownership for Device Memory

What Ownership Covers?

The ownership story of Rust covers the lifetime of device memory completely. The allocation happens in constructors, the release happens in **`Drop`**, double frees are unrepresentable, and leaks require deliberate effort. The sizes are checked on every transfer, as an earlier chapter showed. This is real protection, and we should also say clearly what it does not cover. The ownership rules say nothing about how threads inside a kernel index into a buffer, so coalescing remains our responsibility, and the borrow checker cannot see a strided subscript any more than it can see a race between blocks.

A pair of transpose kernels makes the limit concrete. Our naive version and our padded version, which the project below builds, are identical in every respect the compiler can check, since both own their buffers correctly, both guard their bounds, and both drop cleanly. Yet one will move a fifth of the bandwidth of the other on the same hardware. The type system cannot distinguish them, and no future compiler version will close that gap, because the difference lives in address arithmetic the hardware interprets at run time.

Geometry that Stays

The division of labor is worth stating as a principle, because it recurs in every remaining chapter. In it, Rust manages the existence of GPU memory, and we manage its geometry. The language rules out the crashes and leaks that consume C++ debugging time, which frees our attention for layout, alignment, and access order, the concerns that actually decide throughput. The cuda-oxide safety model from chapter 5 pushes the boundary further inward, and even there, the geometry of access stays ours.

Far from diminishing Rust's contribution, this boundary explains why the language pays off in performance work specifically. A tuning session rearranges subscripts, tiles, and layouts aggressively, and every rearrangement in C++ risks reintroducing the lifetime and bounds bugs that reviews then must chase. With Rust holding the existence guarantees fixed, we refactor geometry with a freedom C++ programmers budget extra review time for, and the transpose project below leans on exactly that freedom through three rewrites of the same kernel.

Matrix Transpose Optimized

Four Kernels

The transpose is the classic vehicle for this chapter because it cannot avoid mixing access patterns, as one side of the copy must cross the matrix grain. Our benchmark transposes a 4096 by 4096 matrix of f32 values, which moves 64 megabytes in and 64 megabytes out per pass, and we will report effective bandwidth as total bytes moved divided by kernel time. A device-to-device copy kernel sets the ceiling, and Harris follows the same protocol in An Efficient Matrix Transpose in CUDA C/C++ on the NVIDIA technical blog.

We will now add four kernels to **kernels/src/lib.rs**:

```
const TILE: usize = 32;


#[kernel]
pub unsafe fn copy_grid(input: &[f32], output: *mut f32, width: usize) {
    let x = (thread::block_idx_x() * thread::block_dim_x() +
thread::thread_idx_x()) as usize;
    let y = (thread::block_idx_y() * thread::block_dim_y() +
thread::thread_idx_y()) as usize;
    if x < width && y < width {
        *output.add(y * width + x) = input[y * width + x];
    }
}


#[kernel]
pub unsafe fn transpose_naive(input: &[f32], output: *mut f32, width:
usize) {
    let x = (thread::block_idx_x() * thread::block_dim_x() +
thread::thread_idx_x()) as usize;
    let y = (thread::block_idx_y() * thread::block_dim_y() +
thread::thread_idx_y()) as usize;
    if x < width && y < width {
        *output.add(x * width + y) = input[y * width + x];
    }
}


#[kernel]
```

```
pub unsafe fn transpose_tiled(input: &[f32], output: *mut f32, width:
usize) {
    let tile = shared_array![f32; TILE * TILE];
    let tx = thread::thread_idx_x() as usize;
    let ty = thread::thread_idx_y() as usize;

    let x = thread::block_idx_x() as usize * TILE + tx;
    let y = thread::block_idx_y() as usize * TILE + ty;
    if x < width && y < width {
        (*tile)[ty * TILE + tx] = input[y * width + x];
    }
    thread::sync_threads();

    let xt = thread::block_idx_y() as usize * TILE + tx;
    let yt = thread::block_idx_x() as usize * TILE + ty;
    if xt < width && yt < width {
        *output.add(yt * width + xt) = (*tile)[tx * TILE + ty];
    }
}

#[kernel]
pub unsafe fn transpose_padded(input: &[f32], output: *mut f32, width:
usize) {
    let tile = shared_array![f32; TILE * (TILE + 1)];
    let tx = thread::thread_idx_x() as usize;
    let ty = thread::thread_idx_y() as usize;

    let x = thread::block_idx_x() as usize * TILE + tx;
    let y = thread::block_idx_y() as usize * TILE + ty;
    if x < width && y < width {
        (*tile)[ty * (TILE + 1) + tx] = input[y * width + x];
    }
    thread::sync_threads();
```

```
    let xt = thread::block_idx_y() as usize * TILE + tx;
    let yt = thread::block_idx_x() as usize * TILE + ty;
    if xt < width && yt < width {
        *output.add(yt * width + xt) = (*tile)[tx * (TILE + 1) + ty];
    }
}
```

The four kernels tell the whole story in about sixty lines. The copy kernel reads and writes with the same coalesced pattern and therefore shows the best this GPU can do for our launch shape. The naive transpose reads coalesced but writes with a stride of 4096 floats. The tiled version stages a 32 by 32 block through shared memory, so both its global read and its global write walk consecutive addresses, and only the shared memory access changes direction. The padded version widens each tile row by one element to defeat bank conflicts, a trick we will explain right after the numbers.

The shared memory machinery deserves a preview here, though its full treatment belongs to chapter 7. The **shared_array!** macro from **cuda_std** reserves a block visible region, every thread of the block deposits one element, and **sync_threads** hold the block at a barrier until all deposits land. Not until then does any thread read a neighbor's value, which is what makes the exchange safe. The unsafe on these kernels now carries a second obligation beyond disjoint writes, namely that our barrier placement is correct.

Verify First

Naturally, correctness precedes speed, and the benchmark verifies the transpose before timing anything. The host fills the input with each element's linear index, runs the padded kernel once, and checks that output[x * width + y] equals input[y * width + x] across a full pass. A fast wrong kernel is worse than a slow right one, because the wrongness spreads into every downstream result. Not until the check passes does the timing loop begin, and the discipline costs one extra launch.

The choice of fill values deserves its sentence as well, because linear indices make every position self describing. When element three million holds the value three million, any misplaced write announces both where it landed and where it came from, and a transpose bug becomes a coordinate we can reason about rather than a vague wrongness. A fill of random values would detect the same errors while explaining none of them, and a fill of zeros would detect almost nothing at all.

The host member times each kernel over twenty iterations after one warm up launch, synchronizes before stopping the clock, and converts elapsed seconds into gigabytes per second. The warm up matters because the driver performs its just in time compilation on first use, as an earlier chapter explained, and timing that first launch would poison the average. No other part of the program is new machinery, since buffers, module loading, and launches all follow an earlier chapter, so we show only the measurement loop.

We will then add the loop to **memory_lab/src/main.rs** as below:

```
let width: usize = 4096;
let grid = ((width / TILE) as u32, (width / TILE) as u32);
let block = (TILE as u32, TILE as u32);
let bytes_moved = 2 * width * width * 4;

for name in ["copy_grid", "transpose_naive", "transpose_tiled",
"transpose_padded"] {
    let func = module.get_function(name)?;

    // warm up
    unsafe {
        launch!(func<<<grid, block, 0, stream>>>(
            d_in.as_device_ptr(), d_in.len(), d_out.as_device_ptr(), width
        ))?;
    }
    stream.synchronize()?;

    let start = Instant::now();
    for _ in 0..20 {
        unsafe {
            launch!(func<<<grid, block, 0, stream>>>(
                d_in.as_device_ptr(), d_in.len(), d_out.as_device_ptr(),
width
            ))?;
        }
    }
    stream.synchronize()?;

    let secs = start.elapsed().as_secs_f64() / 20.0;
    println!("{:<18} {:>5.0} GB/s", name, bytes_moved as f64 / secs /
1e9);
```

```
}
```

Reading Scoreboard

We will now run **`cargo run -p memory_lab`**, and our reference machine produces the chapter's scoreboard:

```
copy_grid            616 GB/s
transpose_naive      129 GB/s
transpose_tiled      441 GB/s
transpose_padded     549 GB/s
```

The table rewards a slow read. The naive kernel keeps barely a fifth of the ceiling, and its only sin is one strided subscript, which is the cost of ignoring coalescing on this hardware. The tiled kernel recovers most of the loss by paying two trips through shared memory in exchange for two coalesced global passes, a trade that wins because shared memory is an order of magnitude faster. The final padding step buys another hundred gigabytes per second with a single constant, and it deserves its own paragraph.

The shared memory on each SM is divided into thirty-two banks, and simultaneous accesses to the same bank serialize. A square 32 by 32 tile places every element of a column into the same bank, so the transposed read of the tile collides thirty-two ways. A row stride widened to thirty-three staggers the columns across the banks, and the collisions vanish at the price of one wasted float per row. The identical fix appears in Harris's transpose write up, and our padded kernel differs from the tiled one by literally a single plus one in two subscripts.

One number in the table deserves a defense before anyone feels shortchanged, namely that even our best kernel stops short of the copy ceiling. The remaining gap belongs to the tile machinery itself, the barrier waits, and the imperfect overlap of reads and writes, and chasing it further would buy single digit percentages at the cost of considerably stranger code. The judgment of when a result is good enough is as much a professional skill as the ability to improve one, and 549 out of 616 is a result we bank with a clear conscience.

The campaign appears as a roadmap in Fig 6.3, and the shape of the numbers matters more than their exact values, which will vary with GPU and driver. Every stage was one idea, one small edit, and one measurement, and that rhythm, change one thing and then measure, is the entire method of a later chapter in miniature. The same discipline will guard us against folklore optimizations that sound clever and move nothing:

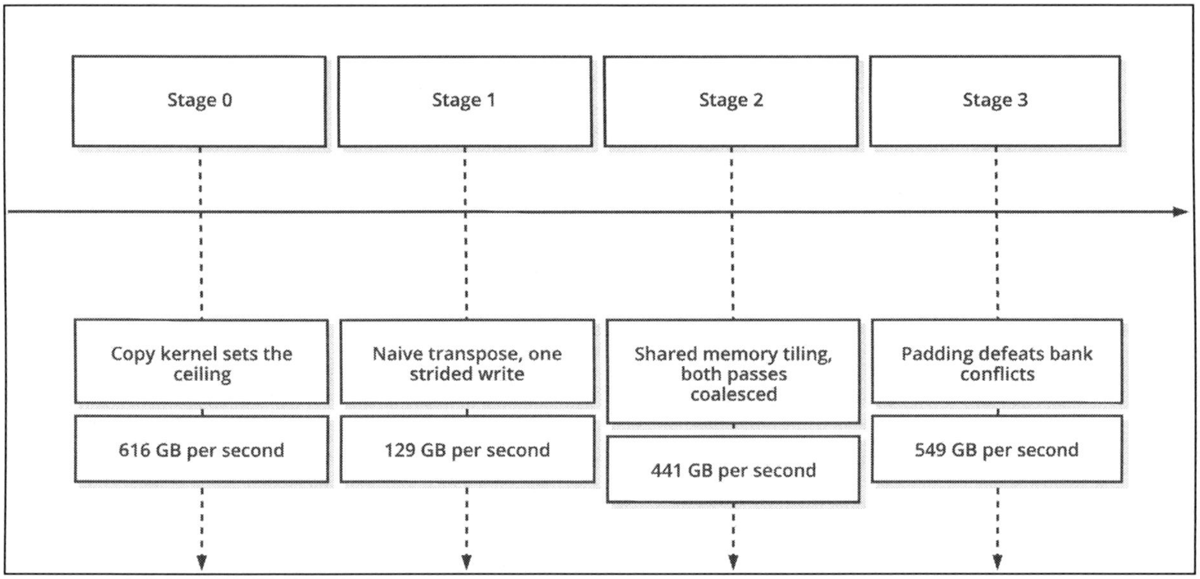

Fig 6.3: Transpose Optimization Roadmap

Our memory has stopped being invisible. We know where our bytes live, why pinned staging doubles transfer speed, how a warp's addresses merge or shatter, and what a strided subscript costs on real silicon, namely four fifths of our bandwidth. The **`memory_lab`** member will keep serving as our bandwidth probe for the rest of the book. In chapter 7, shared memory graduates from a staging trick to a collaboration space, because reductions and scans need threads to combine values, and that requires the synchronization story we have so far only brushed against.

CHAPTER 7
MAKING THREADS COOPERATE

In this chapter, our threads stop working alone. Every kernel so far assigned one element to one thread and kept them strangers, and that pattern, however productive, cannot compute a sum, a minimum, or a running total, because those results need threads to combine values. We will learn the two tools that make combination safe, namely shared memory as a workspace and the block barrier as a traffic signal, and we will build the two patterns that practitioners reuse everywhere, parallel reduction and prefix scan.

The honest theme of an earlier chapter returns with higher stakes, since cooperation creates races that Rust's borrow checker cannot see, and we will name that limitation precisely before writing any code. Our project delivers the routine trio of data tasks, a sum, a minimum and maximum, and a byte histogram, each verified against a CPU pass. The **`kernels`** crate grows again, a member named **`coop_lab`** runs everything, and a timing comparison shows what warp divergence from an earlier chapter cost inside a real algorithm.

Shared Memory

Region per Block

In chapter 6, we used shared memory as a staging area, and the deeper truth is that it is the only memory where threads of a block can converse quickly. The **`shared_array!`** macro reserves a region per block, every thread sees the same addresses, and nothing about the region survives the block's retirement. The capacity is the binding constraint, since an SM offers tens of kilobytes to be divided among its resident blocks, and a greedy allocation reduces how many blocks fit, which trades away the latency hiding of an earlier chapter. Our kernels in this chapter reserve one kilobyte per block, a comfortably modest bite, and the occupancy reports of a later chapter will let us see exactly what any larger appetite would cost.

The third slot in our launch chevrons finally earns its keep. A kernel can declare shared memory statically, as our macros do, or receive a byte budget at launch time through that third argument, which suits kernels whose tile size depends on the data. The two toolchains expose the dynamic form differently, with **`cuda_std`** reading it through a dedicated function and cuda-oxide through **`DynamicSharedArray`**, and we will not need it before a later chapter. What matters now is that the zero we have passed since an earlier chapter was a real resource decision.

The whiteboard image from our section title earns its keep if we take it literally. A team gathered around one board can sketch fast precisely because everyone sees the same surface, and the same closeness creates the same hazard, since two people writing over each other produce nonsense neither intended. All this chapter amounts to the etiquette of that board, namely who writes where, when everyone steps back to look, and when the next round of writing may begin.

Meaningful Barrier

The barrier is what turns shared bytes into shared meaning. A call to **`sync_threads`** hold every thread of the block until all of them arrive, which guarantees that writes before the barrier are visible to reads after it. We will follow two rules to keep barriers safe. Every thread of the block must reach the same barrier, so a barrier inside a divergent branch is a deadlock we hand build. And every crossing of data between threads needs its own barrier, since the hardware promises nothing about timing otherwise. The discipline appears in Fig 7.1:

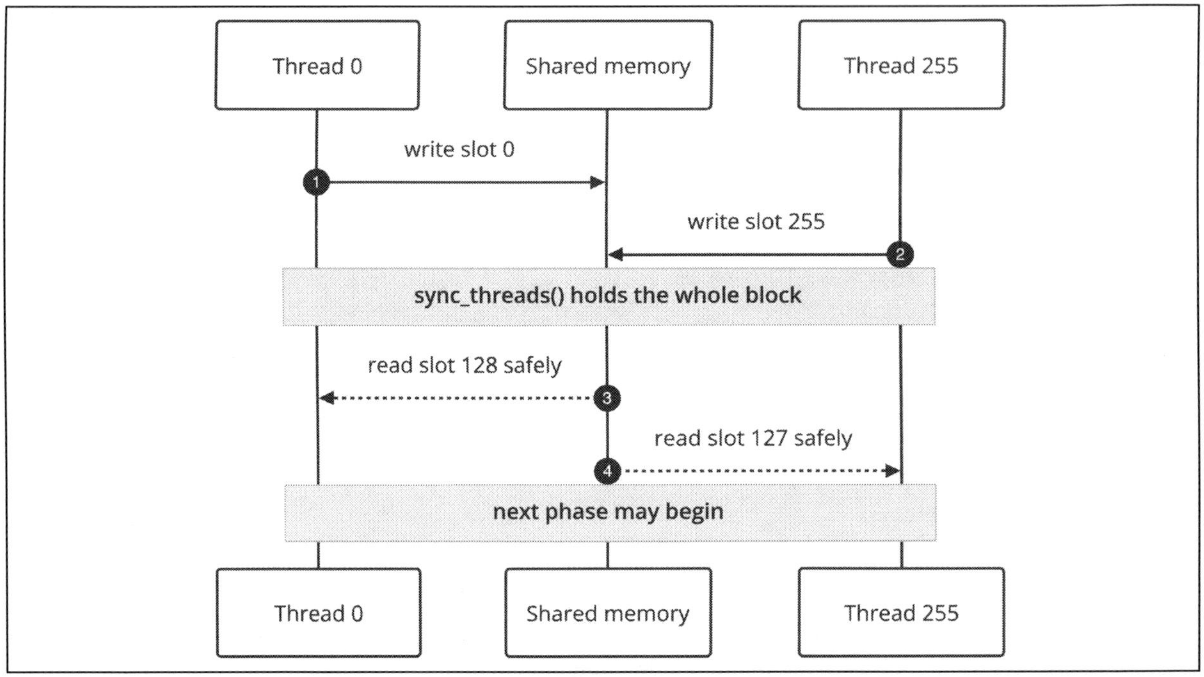

Fig 7.1: Write, Synchronize, Read Discipline

A reassurance belongs beside the two rules, because the barrier scope is narrower than newcomers fear. The call synchronizes one block, never the whole grid, so our barriers cost tens of cycles rather than a device wide stall, and blocks continue to retire independently exactly as an earlier chapter promised. When an algorithm truly needs every block to finish before the next phase, the honest tool is a second kernel launch, and our two-act reduction below demonstrates precisely that structure.

Borrow Checker Challenges

Why Kernels Stay Unsafe?

We should be precise about why this chapter's kernels stay **`unsafe`** in Rust-CUDA. The borrow checker guards aliasing through types, and a shared array is aliased by design, with two hundred fifty-six threads holding what amounts to the same mutable reference. No lifetime annotation expresses the discipline that thread twelve writes slot twelve before the barrier and reads slot one hundred forty after it. The compiler therefore steps back, and the **`unsafe`** block records that the proof of order lives with us, exactly the framing an earlier chapter gave for tier two.

This is a demotion of the compiler, not a dismissal, and the distinction keeps our confidence calibrated. All code outside the shared array remains fully checked, so our slice bounds, our lifetimes, and our host code enjoy every guarantee the earlier chapters celebrated, and the unchecked region shrinks to a few lines around each barrier. The honest accounting is that Rust narrows the search area for cooperation bugs rather than eliminating them, and a narrowed search area is most of what debugging ever needed.

Discipline over Cleverness

Here, discipline scales better than cleverness, and two habits carry the entire chapter. First, we write each kernel as phases separated by barriers, where a phase either writes shared memory or reads it, and never both for the same slots. Second, every **`unsafe`** block earns a comment stating why the access order holds, the practice the cuda-oxide safety chapter recommends, because at two in the morning the comment is the fastest path back to the invariant. The kernels built this way read like little protocols, and protocols can be reviewed.

The topic of testing deserves one more honest sentence, because races laugh at unit tests. A racy kernel can pass a thousand runs on one GPU and fail hourly on another, since the schedule that exposes the bug depends on hardware, driver, and load. The only trustworthy detectors are analysis and instrumentation, namely the phase discipline we adopted above and the compute-sanitizer tool that a later chapter runs against exactly the kernels we are writing now. Until then, our rule is simple, namely that no shared slot is read in the phase that wrote it.

Parallel Reduction

Tree and Two Act Play

A reduction collapses many values into one with an associative operation, and the parallel version is a tree. Each round pairs values and combines them, and the survivors halve until one remains, so a block of 256 values finishes in eight rounds rather than 255 sequential additions. In Optimizing Parallel Reduction in CUDA, Harris walks through seven refinements of this idea, and we will implement the two ends of his spectrum to feel the difference. The tree appears in Fig 7.2 as a flow of values into the final sum:

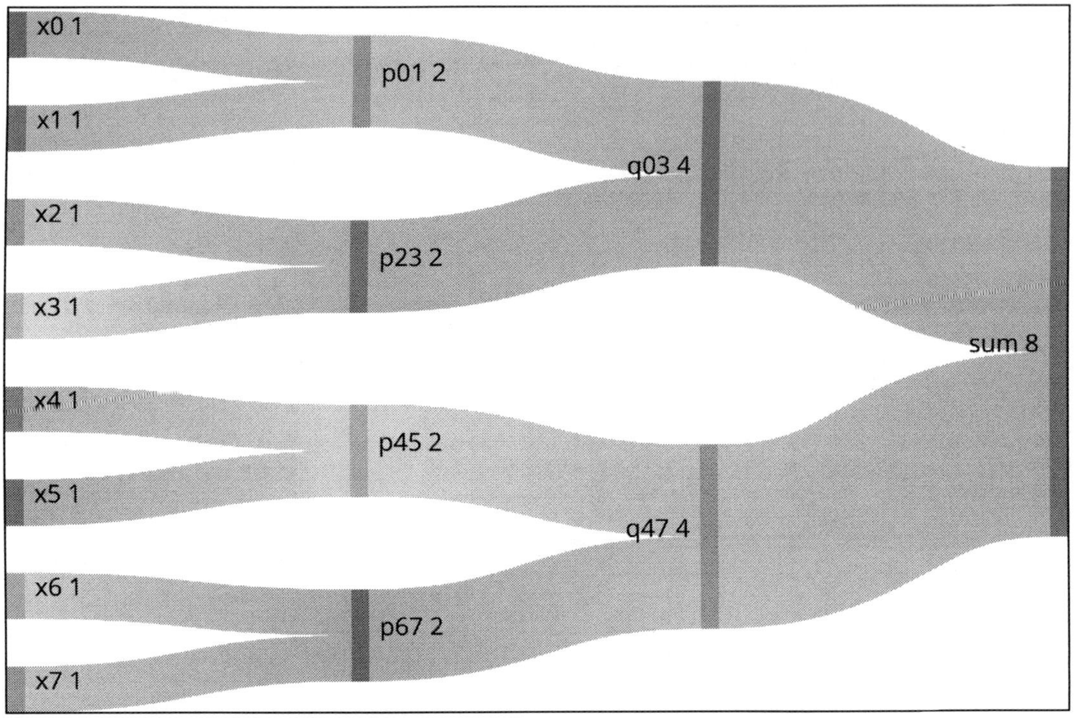

Fig 7.2: Reduction Tree as Flow of Values

One block can only reduce what it can see, so a full reduction is a two-act play. In act one, we launch thousands of blocks, and each write one partial result, which turns sixteen million values into four thousand and ninety six. In act two, we combine the partials, and three respectable options exist, namely a second kernel launch over the partials, a single atomic add per block, or a host side finish. We choose the host finish for its transparency, and a later chapter will quietly switch to the second kernel when the partial array grows.

Divergent vs. Sequential Addressing

We will now add both reduction kernels to **kernels/src/lib.rs**:

```
#[kernel]
pub unsafe fn reduce_sum_divergent(input: &[f32], partial: *mut f32) {
    let smem = shared_array![f32; 256];
    let tid = thread::thread_idx_x() as usize;
    let i = thread::index_1d() as usize;

    // Phase 1: every thread deposits one value.
    (*smem)[tid] = if i < input.len() { input[i] } else { 0.0 };
```

```
    thread::sync_threads();

    // Tree rounds: workers scattered across all warps.
    let mut stride = 1;
    while stride < 256 {
        if tid % (2 * stride) == 0 {
            (*smem)[tid] += (*smem)[tid + stride];
        }
        thread::sync_threads();
        stride *= 2;
    }

    if tid == 0 {
        *partial.add(thread::block_idx_x() as usize) = (*smem)[0];
    }
}

#[kernel]
pub unsafe fn reduce_sum_sequential(input: &[f32], partial: *mut f32) {
    let smem = shared_array![f32; 256];
    let tid = thread::thread_idx_x() as usize;
    let i = thread::index_1d() as usize;

    (*smem)[tid] = if i < input.len() { input[i] } else { 0.0 };
    thread::sync_threads();

    // Tree rounds: workers packed into the lowest warps.
    let mut stride = 128;
    while stride > 0 {
        if tid < stride {
            (*smem)[tid] += (*smem)[tid + stride];
        }
        thread::sync_threads();
```

```
        stride /= 2;
    }

    if tid == 0 {
        *partial.add(thread::block_idx_x() as usize) = (*smem)[0];
    }
}
```

The two kernels differ only in who does the adding. The divergent version keeps the classic shape from older material, where a thread participates when its index is a multiple of the doubling stride, so active threads scatter thinly across every warp, and each warp pays for both branch sides round after round. The sequential version compacts the workers, since threads below the shrinking stride do all the adding, so whole warps retire early and divergence disappears. We will see each version produce one partial sum per block, while the host adds the 4096 partials in microseconds.

Our reference machine reduces sixteen million floats in 1.41 milliseconds with the divergent kernel and 0.79 with the sequential one, a near doubling from reshuffling which thread holds the work. A third refinement lets the last thirty-two values skip shared memory entirely, because warp shuffle instructions move registers between lanes directly, and the warp module of **`cuda_std`** exposes them. We leave that step as guided reading in Harris's write up and in the warp chapter of the cuda-oxide book, since the two toolchains name the intrinsics differently while the idea is identical.

A number this dramatic deserves one sentence of interpretation before we move on. Not one operation of arithmetic changed between the two kernels, since both perform the identical two hundred fifty-five additions per block, and the doubling came entirely from which threads sat idle in which warps. This is an earlier chapter's warp model paying its first cash dividend, and it previews the method of a later chapter, where we will learn to ask the profiler which of our warps are busy rather than guessing from the source code.

Parallel Prefix Scan

From Reduction to Scan

The scan generalizes reduction by keeping every intermediate result, so each output position holds the combination of all inputs up to it. An inclusive scan of 3, 1, 4, 1 yield 3, 4, 8, 9, while the exclusive variant shifts the results right and starts at zero. A running bank balance is the homely version of the same idea, since each line of a statement shows the sum of every deposit up to that moment, and nobody would call a bank statement exotic. The pattern looks sequential by nature and famously is not, as Blelloch showed in his prefix sums work at Carnegie Mellon, and scans now power stream compaction, radix sorts, and memory allocation offsets inside almost every

GPU library we will meet.

Our implementation uses the Hillis and Steele form, which suits block sized inputs and reads clearly. In each round, every position adds the value one stride to its left, the stride doubles, and after log rounds every prefix is complete. The price of clarity is two barriers per round, one protecting the reads and one protecting the writes, and the rounds sit on a time axis in Fig 7.3, which shows how the block marches through them together:

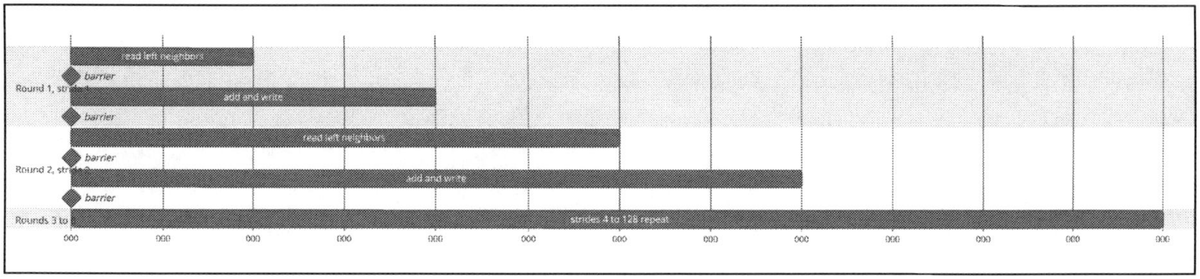

Fig 7.3: One Block Marching through Scan Rounds

Double Barrier

We will then add the scan kernel to **kernels/src/lib.rs**:

```
#[kernel]
pub unsafe fn scan_inclusive(input: &[f32], output: *mut f32) {
    let smem = shared_array![f32; 256];
    let tid = thread::thread_idx_x() as usize;
    let i = thread::index_1d() as usize;

    (*smem)[tid] = if i < input.len() { input[i] } else { 0.0 };
    thread::sync_threads();

    let mut stride = 1;
    while stride < 256 {
        // Phase A: read, protected from this round's writes.
        let addend = if tid >= stride { (*smem)[tid - stride] } else { 0.0
};
        thread::sync_threads();

        // Phase B: write, protected from next round's reads.
```

```
        (*smem)[tid] += addend;
        thread::sync_threads();

        stride *= 2;
    }

    if i < input.len() {
        *output.add(i) = (*smem)[tid];
    }
}
```

The double barrier deserves a close look, because deleting either one produces a kernel that usually works. With only the second barrier, a fast thread can overwrite a slot that a slow neighbor has not yet read, and with only the first, a fast thread can read a slot not yet written, and both corruptions strike rarely and randomly under load. This is the flavor of bug that motivates the whole chapter, invisible to the type system, invisible to small tests, and fatal in production. Our phase discipline from earlier makes both barriers obviously necessary.

A pair of practical footnotes will keep the scan honest. Our kernel scans one block of 256 values, and a longer array composes the same pattern hierarchically, with block sums scanned themselves and added back, a structure we will not need until the pipeline chapters and therefore leave as a cited pattern in Blelloch's treatment. And an exclusive scan needs no second kernel, since a right shift of the inclusive result by one slot during the final write produces it for free.

The verification for the scan also differs from our earlier checks in one instructive way, because a scan error compounds rather than staying local. When position ninety goes wrong, every later position inherits the mistake, so the CPU comparison pinpoints the first divergence rather than merely counting failures, and that first index usually names the guilty round directly. A stride of thirty two as the first bad distance, for instance, points a steady finger at the round where warp boundaries begin to matter.

Sum, Min/Max, and Histogram

One Tree and Three Results

The project member **`coop_lab`** wires the patterns into the routine tasks that real programs need. The sum uses our sequential reduction, the minimum and maximum reuse the identical tree with the combining operation swapped, and the histogram introduces one truly new tool, the atomic addition. All three verify against a plain CPU pass over the same data, in the tradition every chapter has kept. The reduction kernels return per block partials, and the host finishes the last four thousand values itself, a split that keeps the kernels simple at no measurable cost.

These three tasks earn their place by ubiquity rather than glamour. A sum stands behind every average, loss function, and checksum we will ever compute, the extremes drive normalization and outlier checks, and histograms feed everything from image equalization to the bucketing decisions inside sorting libraries. When these three run correctly at memory speed from Rust, a wide shelf of everyday analytics becomes ours without further invention, which is exactly the kind of quiet capability this book is assembling chapter by chapter.

The minimum and maximum kernels demonstrate a satisfying property of the reduction tree, namely that the algorithm and the operation are independent. We copy the sequential sum kernel, replace the addition with a comparison, and seed the out-of-range slots with infinity instead of zero, and nothing else changes, not the barriers, not the strides, not the host finish. In a later refactor, a generic kernel over a combining closure could collapse the three into one, and as an earlier chapter showed, cuda-oxide's monomorphization would pay no runtime cost for it.

Histogram and Its Atomics

So here, we will add the histogram kernel with its atomic update:

```
use core::sync::atomic::{AtomicU32, Ordering};

#[kernel]
pub unsafe fn histogram16(input: &[u8], bins: *mut u32) {
    let i = thread::index_1d() as usize;
    if i < input.len() {
        let bin = (input[i] >> 4) as usize;
        let slot = &*(bins.add(bin) as *const AtomicU32);
        slot.fetch_add(1, Ordering::Relaxed);
    }
}
```

An atomic operation is the third way threads may touch common data, beside private slots and barrier separated phases. The fetch and add executes as one indivisible hardware action, so two hundred colliding increments serialize safely instead of dropped updates, and no barrier is involved. They shine when collisions are rare and sting when a single location becomes crowded, which is why our histogram of sixteen bins works while a histogram of two bins would crawl. Later, we meet the same trade inside library code.

A real histogram kernel often adds one more layer, a private histogram per block in shared memory, with threads updating the private copy atomically and one final merge into the global bins per block. The privatization multiplies the number of update targets by the number of blocks, which spreads collisions thin, and NVIDIA's best practices material documents the technique for crowded distributions. Our uniform bytes across sixteen bins stay uncrowded enough that the plain version already runs at memory speed, so we keep the simple form and name the upgrade.

Verification and Cost of Divergence

We will now run **cargo run -p coop_lab**, and our reference machine reports all three tasks:

```
sum:  8391034.0 (GPU) vs 8391033.5 (CPU)   -> verified within 1e-5
min:  0.000    max: 0.999                  -> verified exactly
hist: 16 bins, total 16777216              -> verified bin for bin
divergent reduce:  1.41 ms   sequential reduce: 0.79 ms
```

One verification detail deserves its own sentence, because it will save someone a confused evening. The GPU sum and the CPU sum disagree in the last digits, and both are right, since floating point addition is not associative and the tree combines values in a different order than the sequential loop. Our check therefore accepts a relative difference of one part in a hundred thousand, and the min, max, and histogram comparisons stay exact because their operations are order proof.

This tolerance question follows every parallel float computation we will ever ship, so the habit of deciding it consciously starts here. A tolerance chosen too tight fails honest kernels on reordering noise, while one chosen too loose waves real bugs through, and the right width comes from the data's magnitude and the depth of the combining tree. We will meet the same decision again later when GEMM results face their reference, and the reasoning we practiced on a humble sum transfer without change.

The verification lines close the loop, and the histogram invites one last picture. Our input bytes were drawn uniformly, and the sixteen bins each collect close to one sixteenth of sixteen million samples, which Fig 7.4 shows briefly. The picture is not the proof, the equality check is, but a corrupted bin shows up in it instantly during development. A dropped update from a broken atomic would dent one wedge visibly, and a systematic indexing error would empty a bin outright, so the chart doubles as a coarse diagnostic that costs nothing to keep. In practice, teams chart exactly such sanity views in their pipelines for the same reason, namely that eyes catch gross wrongness faster than they read totals:

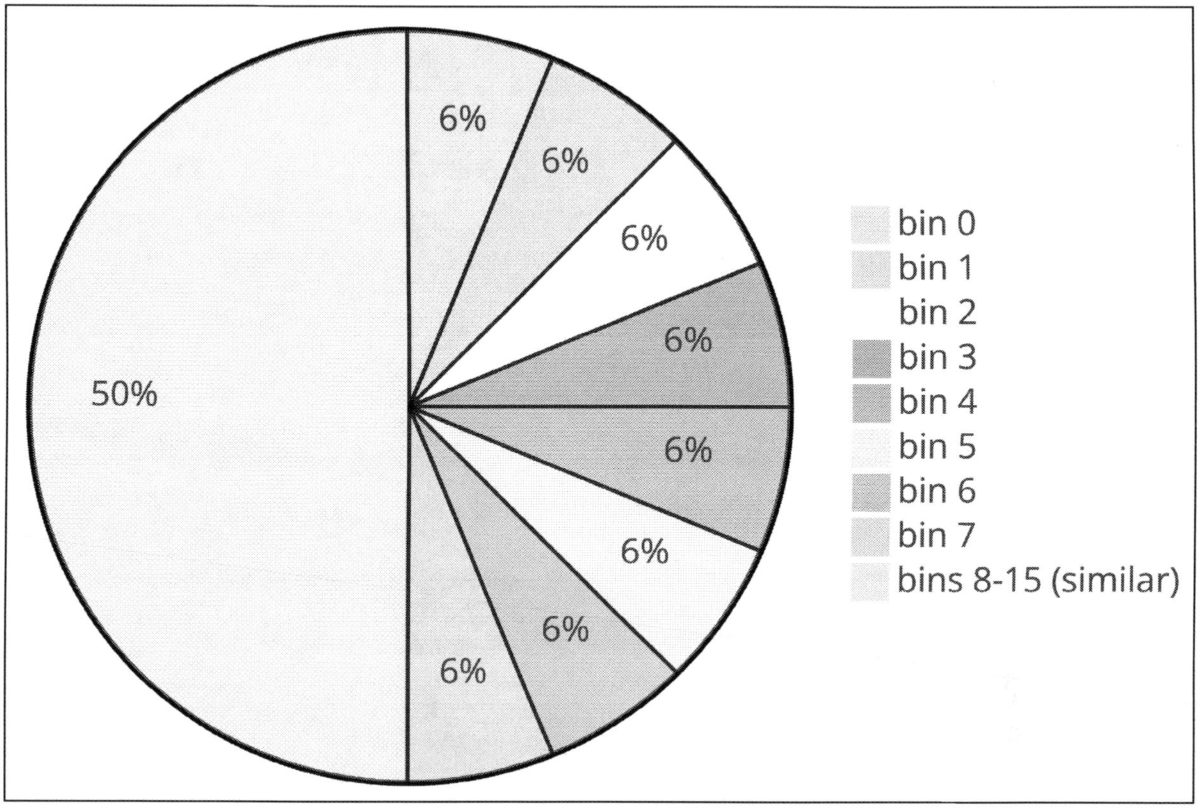

Fig 7.4: Sixteen Uniform Bins

Our vocabulary now includes cooperation. We can stage data on the block whiteboard, march threads through barrier separated phases, collapse millions of values through a tree, keep every prefix with a scan, and let atomics absorb rare collisions, and each technique carried its verification with it. The borrow checker sat this chapter out, and our comments and phase discipline stood in for it honestly, with the sanitizer of a later chapter waiting to audit the arrangement by machine. In chapter 8, we widen the lens from one kernel to whole pipelines, because streams, events, and async Rust decide whether the GPU, however busy inside each kernel, ever waits between them for work.

CHAPTER 8
KEEPING GPU BUSY

In this chapter, we stop measuring single kernels and start choreographing whole workloads, because a GPU spends shocking amounts of time idle in naive programs. The hardware contains separate engines for copying and computing, and they can all run at once, yet every program we have written so far uses exactly one of them at a time. We will learn to overlap transfers with computation using multiple streams, to time GPU work honestly with events, and to keep the pinned memory from an earlier chapter earning its keep.

The chapter then crosses into territory where Rust offers something CUDA C++ simply lacks. The cuda-oxide toolchain models GPU work as lazy **`DeviceOperation`** values that compose like iterators and complete like futures, so an ordinary tokio application can await a kernel exactly as it awaits a network response. Our project builds a two-stream pipeline that brightens half a gigabyte of image data, and the overlapped version will finish in roughly half the time of the serial baseline, a claim the measurement section makes precise.

Cost of Doing One Thing at Time

Three Engines, One in Use

A modern GPU is closer to a small team than a single worker. Beside the compute engine that runs kernels, the card carries dedicated copy engines, direct memory access units that move data across PCIe without any help from the SMs, and our RTX 3080 has one for each direction. In NVIDIA's CUDA Concurrency material, Rennich lays out this machinery, and the consequence is plain. While a kernel computes, an upload and a download could both be in flight, and in our programs so far, they never were.

Our earlier pipeline was honest but wasteful, since the upload, the kernel, and the download stood in single file, and two of the three engines watched the third work. The waste grows with data size, and for workloads where transfers dominate, the serial arrangement can leave most of the wall clock on the table. We can view both schedules for the workload our project will run in Fig 8.1, where the overlapped bars below the serial ones capture the entire thesis of this chapter:

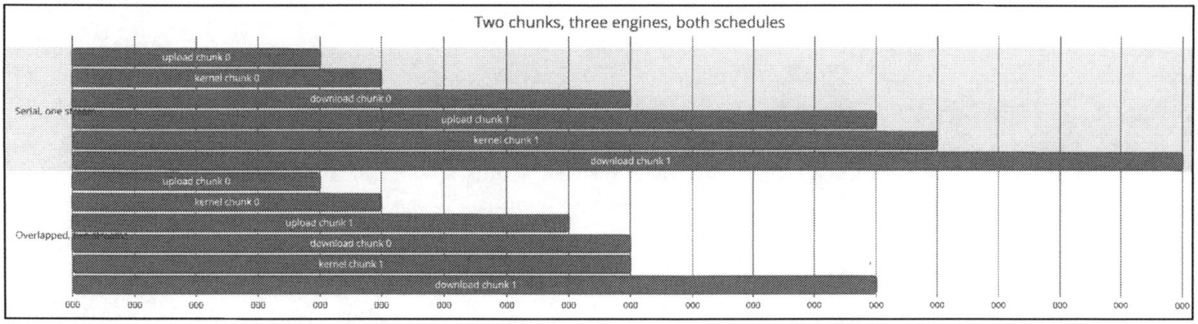

Fig 8.1: Serial vs. Overlapped Schedules

Watching Idleness

A skeptic can watch the idleness directly. Later, we will capture Nsight Systems timelines where the serial pipeline appears as three colored bars taking turns above an idle row for each unused engine, and one screenshot of that staircase converts more engineers than any paragraph. Until then, arithmetic makes the case. Our earlier numbers put a half gigabyte upload near twenty-one milliseconds and the brighten kernel near two, so a serial run spends over ninety percent of its life copying, and every one of those milliseconds is overlappable.

The kitchen of a busy restaurant makes the schedule intuitive before any code does. A cook who fetches ingredients, cooks a dish, and delivers the plate before touching the next order serves a slow dinner, while a kitchen where the runner fetches for table two during table one's cooking serves twice the seats with the same staff. Our copy engines are the runners, the SMs are the stove, and streams are simply the order slips that keep the kitchen honest about sequencing.

Streams and Events in Practice

Dealing Work across Streams

The stream machinery from an earlier chapter turns out to be the whole scheduling interface. The work within one stream runs in submission order, streams are independent of each other, and the hardware engines pull from any stream with eligible work. A second stream in cust costs one line to create, and nothing else about our host code changes shape. The craft lies in dealing work across the streams so that one stream's copy can run under another stream's kernel, which is the pattern the project implements. Not one detail of the launches, the buffers, or the error handling changes when a second stream appears, and this continuity is why the chapter can focus entirely on choreography.

A natural question is how many streams to create, and the honest number is smaller than most first guesses. We find that two streams already unlock copy compute overlap, three cover both copy directions plus compute, and beyond the number of hardware engines the extra streams only add scheduling choice rather than parallel capacity. The NVIDIA concurrency material suggests matching the structure of the workload rather than the specifications of the card, and our pipeline uses two because its pattern has two independent lanes of work.

Events as Clocks

Now, events give us honest clocks for this new world. An event is a marker dropped into a stream, the device stamps it when the preceding work completes, and the elapsed time between two stamps measures pure GPU activity with no host noise. Our **`Instant`** timings so far bundled driver overhead and host scheduling into every number, which was fine for bandwidth tables and becomes misleading once work overlaps. The events also serve as dependencies, since one stream can be told to wait for an event recorded on another, a tool a later chapter will need.

So here, we will time a launch with a pair of events as below:

```
use cust::event::{Event, EventFlags};

let start = Event::new(EventFlags::DEFAULT)?;
let stop = Event::new(EventFlags::DEFAULT)?;

start.record(&stream)?;
// ... launches and async copies on this stream ...
stop.record(&stream)?;

stop.synchronize()?;
let device_ms = stop.elapsed_time_f32(&start)?;
```

The pattern reads like stopwatch usage, and the synchronize on the stop event replaces the stream wide synchronize we have used since an earlier chapter, and it waits only for the marker itself. From here on, our measurements inside pipelines use event time for device work and **`Instant`** only for end-to-end wall clock, and the habit of reporting both catches mysteries early, because a gap between the two numbers points at the host side. The event clock also offers sub millisecond resolution, which our two millisecond kernels will appreciate.

A short vocabulary note prevents a common confusion between the two waiting verbs we now own. A stream synchronize holds the host until everything queued on that stream completes, while an event synchronize holds only until the marker's own moment passes, and work queued after the marker keeps flowing undisturbed. The distinction hardly matters in a serial program and becomes the whole game in an overlapped one, where a carelessly broad wait can quietly re-serialize a pipeline, we worked hard to parallelize.

Overlapping Transfers with Compute

Three Necessary Ingredients

We will combine three ingredients to make overlap real rather than theoretical. The host buffers must be pinned, because the asynchronous copy functions fall back to synchronous behavior on pageable memory and do so silently, which is the single most common reason an overlapped pipeline mysteriously runs at serial speed. The copies must use the asynchronous variants tied to a stream. And the work must be chunked, since overlap needs at least two pieces in flight, one copying while the other computes.

Each ingredient fails in its own accent, and knowing the accents saves diagnostic time. A missing pin produces correct results at serial speed with no warning anywhere, a synchronous copy on an otherwise perfect pipeline serializes just one edge and shaves the speedup rather than erasing it, and an unchunked workload simply has nothing to overlap however many streams we open. When a pipeline underperforms, we audit the three in that order, because the silent one is the likeliest and the cheapest to check.

Chunked Card Deal

The chunked pattern deals the pieces across two streams like cards. The first chunk's upload starts on stream zero, and while its kernel runs, the second chunk's upload proceeds on stream one, and by the middle of the run every engine has work on every beat.

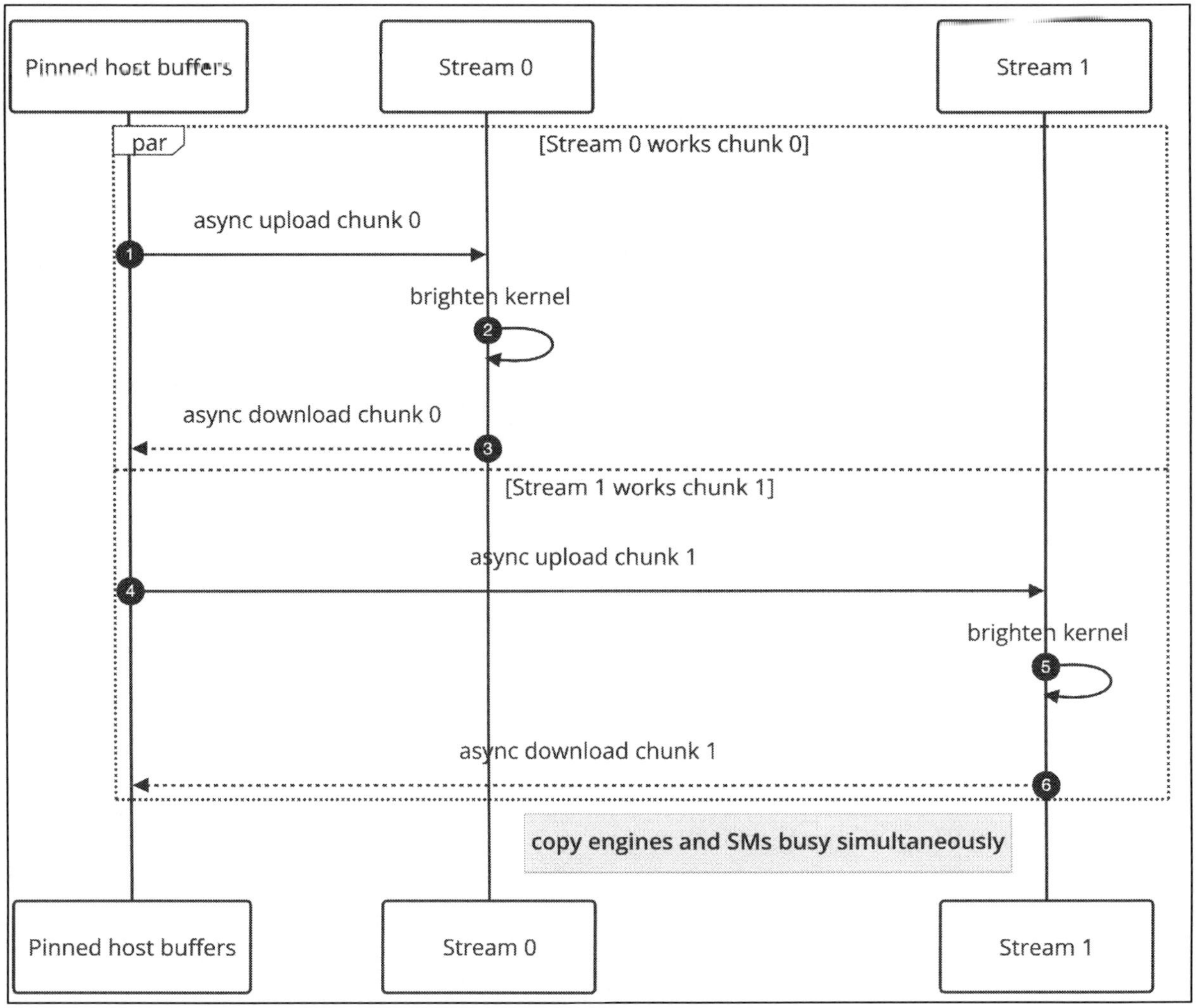

Fig 8.2: Streams Sharing Engines

The asynchronous copy in **`cust`** is marked unsafe for a familiar reason, namely that the call returns while the transfer is still reading our pinned buffer, and we must not touch that buffer until the stream says so. One full round plays out in Fig 8.2:

The deal generalizes past two streams without changing character, which is why the card metaphor earns its place. With three chunks in flight, one can upload while a second computes and a third downloads, saturating all three engines on every beat, and the modulo arithmetic in our project loop extends to any stream count by changing one constant. The returns diminish once every engine has steady work, exactly as the stream counting discussion predicted, so we deal only as many hands as the hardware has players.

GPU Work as Async Rust

Lazy Operations and Stream Pools

All of the above is classic CUDA discipline with Rust types, and now cuda-oxide raises the abstraction. Its **`cuda_launch_async!`** macro returns a DeviceOperation, a lazy description of GPU work that has not touched any stream yet, and the documentation's analogy is worth borrowing, since the operation is a recipe card and a stream is the kitchen that eventually cooks it. The composition happens before any scheduling, so a function can return upload, then multiply, then activate as one value, and the caller decides where and when it runs.

The laziness is the feature to sit with, because it inverts a habit every prior chapter built. Until now, each line of host code fired GPU work the moment it executed, and the shape of our program was the shape of the schedule. With operations as values, description and execution separate cleanly, so a library can hand back sophisticated pipelines without ever touching a stream, and the application composes and runs them under its own policy. This is the same separation that made iterators feel liberating in ordinary Rust.

One setup call stands before any async work, since the runtime needs kitchens to assign. The **`init_device_contexts`** function builds a pool of streams on a chosen device, and the scheduling policy hands them to operations as execution contexts, each carrying the device, the stream, and the CUDA context together. No detail of the pool leaks into the operations themselves, which is the entire point, and a swap from a one stream pool to an eight stream pool changes concurrency without touching a single pipeline definition.

Four Verbs and Combinators

We can reach for four verbs to execute a recipe, in rising order of manual control. The **`sync`** method picks a stream from a pool and blocks until done, which suits tests and scripts. The **`await`** keyword converts the operation into a future inside a tokio runtime, and the task yields instead of blocking. The **`sync_on`** method runs on a stream we supply, and the unsafe **`async_on`** submits without waiting, the fire and forget form that batches many operations before one synchronize. The async chapters at **nvlabs.github.io/cuda-oxide** document all four with their trade offs.

We will now see the awaited form in its natural tokio habitat:

```
#[tokio::main]
```

```
async fn main() -> Result<(), Box<dyn std::error::Error>> {
    init_device_contexts(0, 2)?; // device 0, pool of 2 streams

    let result = cuda_launch_async! {
        kernel: brighten,
        module: module,
        config: LaunchConfig::for_num_elems(n as u32),
        args: [slice(input_dev), 1.5f32, slice_mut(output_dev)]
    }
    .await?;

    Ok(())
}
```

The combinators turn single operations into pipelines. The **`and_then`** combinator feeds one operation's output into the next, **`zip!`** runs two operations and returns both results, **`value`** lifts a plain host value into the pipeline so configurations can ride beside transfers, and **`with_context`** defers construction until the stream is known, the escape hatch for raw driver calls such as asynchronous allocation. If this feels like Iterator and Future had a child, that is the design intent, and the composition costs nothing until execution.

Why Bridge Matters?

A brief look sideways shows why this section matters for the book's thesis. On the C++ side, CUDA offers streams and callbacks but no future abstraction, so the composition of GPU stages with network and file stages means hand rolled state machines. The async story in Python stops at the GIL boundary, where GPU calls block worker threads inside libraries. Meanwhile, Rust arrived with a mature async ecosystem, and cuda-oxide plugs GPU work into it natively, which makes servers that interleave inference with request handling feel like ordinary tokio applications. Later, we build exactly such a shape.

The bridge between hardware and the async runtime deserves its picture, because it is where cuda-oxide is quietly clever. The **`await`** on an operation submits the GPU work and enqueues a host callback on the same stream through **`cuLaunchHostFunc`**, and stream ordering guarantees the callback fires only after the kernel finishes. The callback wakes the parked task, the runtime re polls, and the future reports ready. No thread spins and no thread sleeps on our behalf, so hundreds of GPU tasks can share one runtime. The future's three states appear in Fig 8.3:

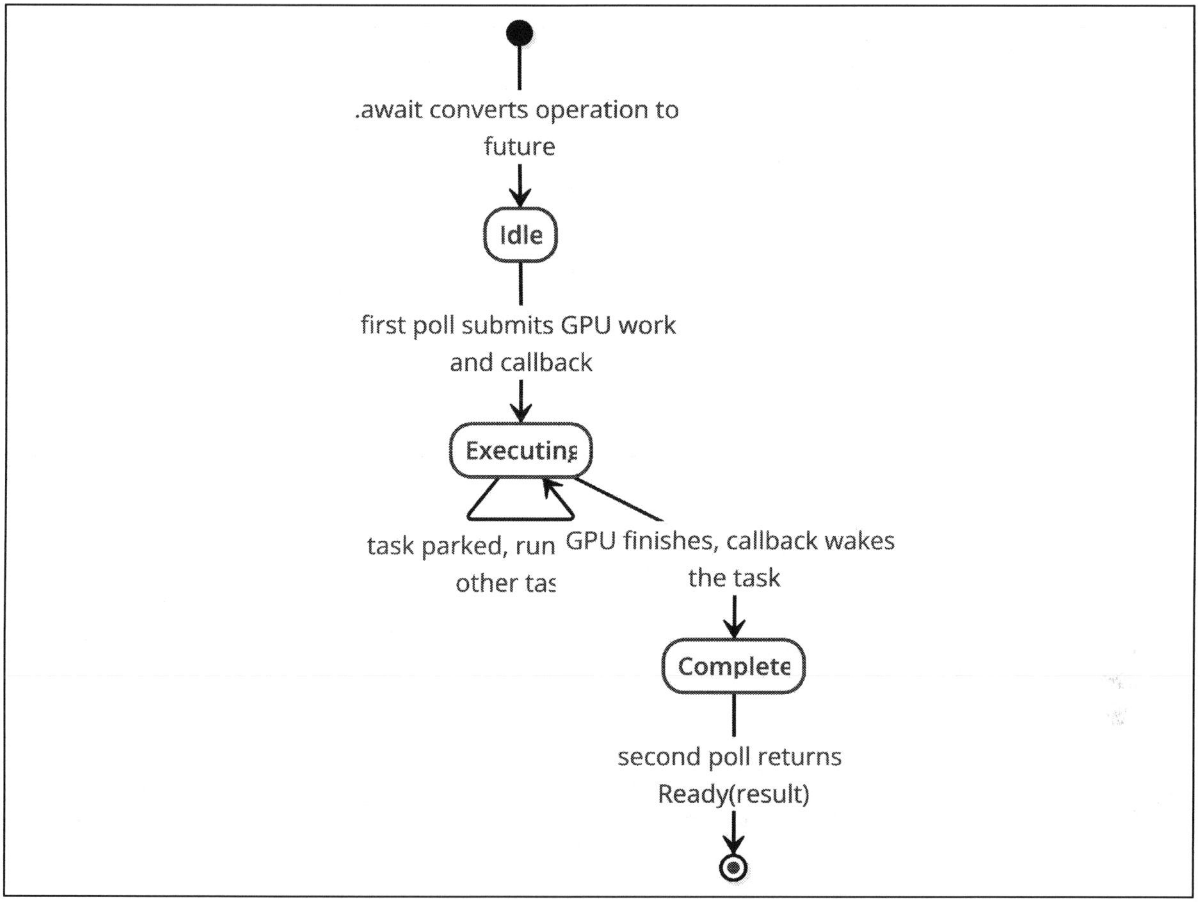

Fig 8.3: Life of DeviceFuture

Our honesty labels apply unchanged. The **DeviceOperation** model lives in the alpha cuda-oxide stack, so we treat it as the preview of where Rust GPU programming is heading, and the classic stream discipline above remains the dependable everyday tool. Happily, the two teach the same concepts, since a scheduling policy is a choice of streams either way, and a move between them is a change of syntax rather than of mental model. Later, the capstone commits to the async style, with this chapter as its foundation.

Two-Stream Data Pipeline

Fair Baseline

The project member **stream_pipeline** puts numbers behind the promises. The workload brightens 512 megabytes of image bytes with the kernel from earlier, split into sixteen chunks of 32 megabytes, and the data rides in pinned buffers end to end. A serial run processes chunks one at a time on a single stream, and the overlapped run deals them across two streams with asynchronous copies in both directions. The events time the device work, **`Instant`** times the wall clock, and the same verification as an earlier chapter checks every output byte.

The serial baseline deserves care, because a sloppy baseline flatters the result. Ours uses the same pinned buffers, the same chunk size, and the same kernel as the overlapped run, and it differs in exactly one respect, namely that every operation queues on a single stream. Any speedup we report therefore comes from overlap alone rather than from pinning or chunking, which the baseline already enjoys. A fair baseline is half of honest benchmarking, and a later chapter elevates the habit into a checklist.

Overlapped Loop

So here, we will build the overlapped loop inside **stream_pipeline/src/main.rs** as below:

```
let streams = [
    Stream::new(StreamFlags::NON_BLOCKING, None)?,
    Stream::new(StreamFlags::NON_BLOCKING, None)?,
];
let mut d_in = [
    DeviceBuffer::<u8>::zeroed(CHUNK)?,
    DeviceBuffer::<u8>::zeroed(CHUNK)?,
];
let mut d_out = [
    DeviceBuffer::<u8>::zeroed(CHUNK)?,
    DeviceBuffer::<u8>::zeroed(CHUNK)?,
];

for chunk in 0..NUM_CHUNKS {
    let s = chunk % 2;
    let offset = chunk * CHUNK;
    let stream = &streams[s];

    // SAFETY: pinned_in/pinned_out outlive both streams, and no
    // region is reused before its stream synchronizes below.
    unsafe {
        d_in[s].async_copy_from(&pinned_in[offset..offset + CHUNK],
stream)?;
```

```
        launch!(brighten<<<grid, block, 0, stream>>>(
            d_in[s].as_device_ptr(),
            d_in[s].len(),
            1.5f32,
            d_out[s].as_device_ptr()
        ))?;

        d_out[s].async_copy_to(&mut pinned_out[offset..offset + CHUNK],
stream)?;
    }
}
streams[0].synchronize()?;
streams[1].synchronize()?;
```

The loop deserves two remarks. The device buffers exist per stream rather than per chunk, so the pipeline reuses two upload buffers and two download buffers for the whole run, which keeps device memory flat regardless of data size. And the unsafe blocks around the asynchronous copies carry the buffer liveness obligation, which our structure discharges trivially, since the pinned buffers outlive both streams and nothing writes a region until its stream synchronizes. The SAFETY comments state exactly that.

The modulo arithmetic on the loop counter is doing quiet scheduling work worth noticing. Because it steers even chunks to stream zero and odd chunks to stream one, the loop guarantees that consecutive chunks always occupy different streams, which is exactly the adjacency the overlap needs, and it reuses each stream's buffers only after a full round trip. No clever scheduler sits anywhere in this program, and the entire choreography of Fig 8.2 falls out of one remainder operation and the ordering rules that streams already promised us.

Reading Speedup

We will now run **`cargo run -p stream_pipeline`**, and our reference machine settles the claim:

```
serial:      46.8 ms wall   45.9 ms device
overlapped: 24.9 ms wall   24.1 ms device
speedup:     1.88x          verification: every byte matches
```

The speedup lands where the engine arithmetic predicts. Our workload moves a gigabyte in total across PCIe while computing for barely two milliseconds, so the serial time is essentially upload plus download, and the overlapped time collapses toward whichever direction is longer, since the two copy engines run simultaneously and the kernel hides entirely under them. A compute heavy workload would show a smaller transfer win but hide more kernel time instead, and a later chapter exercises exactly that balance.

The close agreement between wall time and device time in both rows also deserves a nod, because it certifies the host code itself. A pipeline whose wall clock ran well ahead of its event clock would be confessing that the CPU side, perhaps an allocation inside the loop or a debug print, had become the bottleneck while the GPU waited politely. Our loop allocates nothing and prints nothing until the end, and the two clocks agreeing within a millisecond is the receipt for that discipline.

One failure mode is worth rehearsing before we celebrate. If we swap the pinned buffers for ordinary vectors, the program still runs and still verifies, but the asynchronous copies quietly degrade to synchronous ones and the overlapped time creeps back toward the serial number. The rule from an earlier chapter thus returns with teeth, since pinning was optional for correctness and is mandatory for concurrency. A five line experiment confirms it, and we encourage that experiment once in person, because a regression we have watched with our own eyes is a regression we will recognize instantly when a refactor reintroduces it two months from now.

The GPU no longer waits for us. We can time device work with device clocks, keep every engine fed with chunked streams, and, through cuda-oxide, hand whole GPU pipelines to an async runtime as ordinary awaitable values. The pipeline member joins our workspace as the template for every overlapped design to come, and its SAFETY comments, its fair baseline, and its two clock report are as much a part of the template as its loop. In chapter 9, the kernels themselves finally grow teeth, because matrix multiplication gives the compute engine enough work to be worth scheduling around, and cuBLAS sets a ceiling that will keep us humble in the most instructive possible way.

CHAPTER 9
DELIVERING REAL MATH

In this chapter, our GPU finally gets work worthy of its silicon. The matrix multiply is the exercise on which every platform, every library, and every accelerator generation is judged, and we will treat it as our benchmark of record. We will write a naive GEMM in Rust, rebuild it with shared memory tiling, and then call cuBLAS to learn what the ceiling looks like, with trillions of floating point operations per second measured at every step. The honest gaps between those three numbers teach more than any single kernel could.

The chapter ends with the scoreboard this book promised earlier. We will hold our Rust kernels against their CUDA C++ twins compiled from the same algorithms, and hold Rust calling cuBLAS against Python calling the same library through CuPy. The results preview the book's larger argument, namely that the language writing the kernel matters less than the algorithm, and the language calling the library barely matters at all. A new member named **`gemm_bench`** joins the workspace and runs every measurement.

GEMM as Benchmark of Record

Arithmetic Intensity and Roofline

The general matrix multiply, GEMM in library speak, earns its throne through arithmetic intensity. A multiplication of two n by n matrices performs two n cubed operations while touching only three n squared values, so at n equal to 4096 every loaded number can participate in thousands of operations. Meanwhile, workloads like our vector addition offer the memory system one addition per load and are doomed to run at bandwidth speed, while GEMM offers enough reuse to approach the arithmetic peak. In Communications of the ACM in 2009, Williams, Waterman, and Patterson formalized this spectrum as the roofline model.

The roofline image is worth carrying in our heads for the rest of the book, because it prices every kernel before we write it. The picture is a shed roof, with a sloped section where bandwidth caps performance and a flat section where arithmetic does, and each kernel hangs under the roof at the horizontal position its reuse per byte earns. Our chapters so far lived entirely on the slope, and GEMM is our first genuine visit to the flat, which is why the numbers in this chapter finally carry the word teraflops.

The benchmark of record status is not vanity, since GEMM sits inside almost everything this book's audience ships. The dense layers and attention blocks in neural networks are GEMM calls, the convolutions of computer vision lower to GEMM through im2col, and recommender factorizations and graphics transforms reduce to it as well. When hardware vendors quote deep learning performance, they are largely quoting GEMM. A platform that multiplies matrices well earns credibility everywhere else, which is why our later pipeline will spend most of its device time inside the kernels and calls this chapter builds. The hours we spend here repay themselves across every workload that follows, because a mental model of GEMM performance transfers to any kernel with reuse to exploit.

The intensity only pays if we exploit the reuse, and that is the entire craft. A naive kernel rereads each matrix element from global memory thousands of times and turns a compute problem back into a bandwidth problem, while tiling parks blocks of the matrices in shared memory where the reuse becomes nearly free. In Benchmarking GPUs to Tune Dense Linear Algebra at SC 2008, Volkov and Demmel wrote the classic tour of these trade offs. Our benchmarks so far take their places on the intensity map in Fig 9.1:

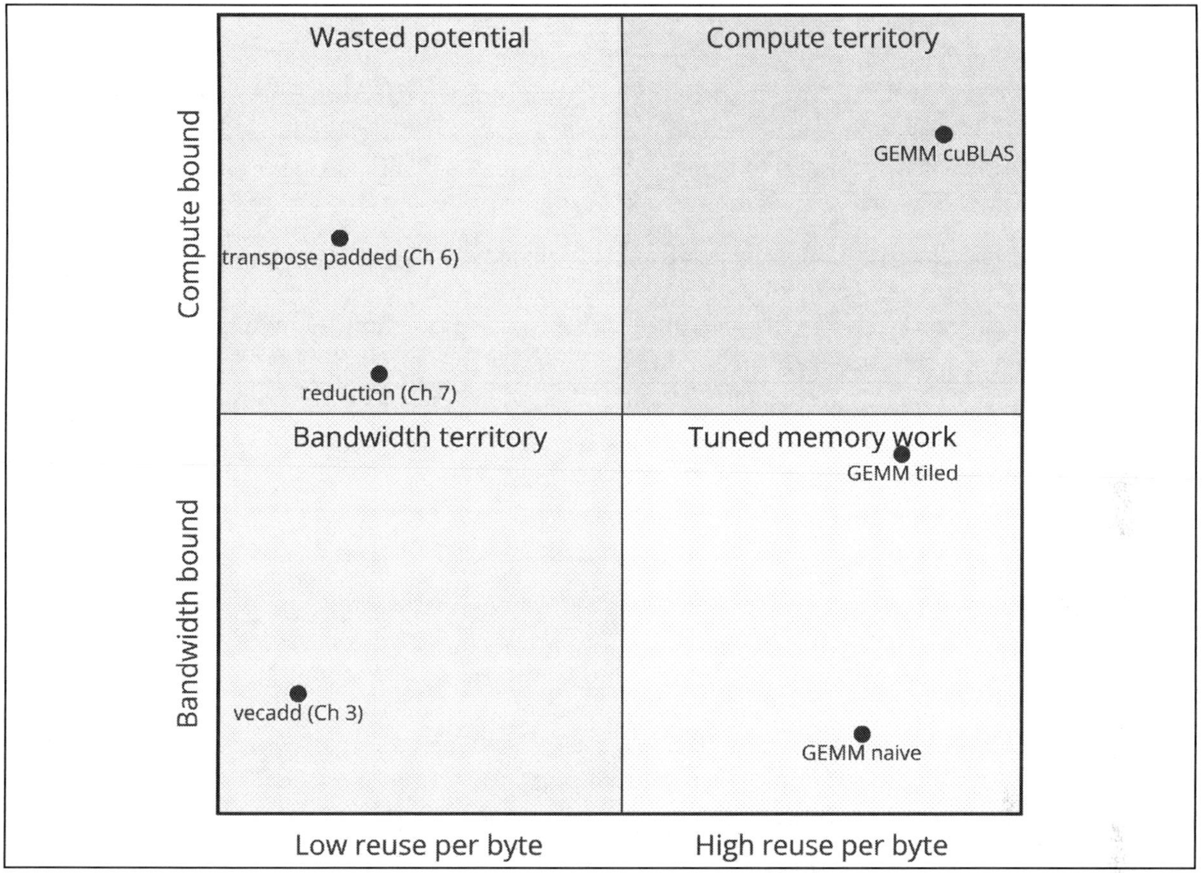

Fig 9.1: Workloads on Intensity Map

The expectations deserve numbers before we run anything. Our RTX 3080 lists a theoretical FP32 peak near thirty trillion operations per second, and its memory system feeds 760 gigabytes per second, so any kernel below an intensity of roughly forty operations per byte lives under the bandwidth roof. The naive kernel should land under one teraflop, the tiled version should multiply that severalfold, and cuBLAS should reach a large fraction of peak. The habit of guessing before measuring is what turns benchmarks into understanding.

Protocol and Launch Geometry

Our protocol stays honest in three ways. First, we verify every kernel at n equal to 512 against a plain CPU triple loop before any timing, and we also cross check the fast kernels against cuBLAS at full size within a relative tolerance, since floating point summation order differs as an earlier chapter explained. Second, the timing uses events from chapter 8, with twenty iterations after a warm up launch. Third, the reported figure is operations per second computed from two n cubed at n equal to 4096, the convention every GEMM paper shares.

The launch geometry reuses an earlier chapter without surprises, and a short recap saves a page flip. The blocks are 32 by 32, the same shape as our transpose work, and the grid is 128 by 128 for the full 4096 dimension, which places sixteen thousand blocks over sixty-eight SMs and leaves the scheduler saturated. One thread owns one output element in both hand written kernels, so the guard question disappears when the dimension divides the tile evenly, and our benchmark fixes n at a multiple of thirty-two for exactly that reason, a simplification we flag now so nobody mistakes it for a general rule.

One workspace note keeps the project connected to its family. The member **`gemm_bench`** follows the layout of **`memory_lab`** from an earlier chapter, with the kernels living in the shared **`kernels`** crate and the host handling data, timing, and verification, so nothing structural is new. The only fresh dependency is **`cublas-sys`** for the library rows of the scoreboard, and its linking rides on the same environment variables we wired earlier. A reader who has built every chapter so far will build this one without ceremony.

Naive Kernel

One Thread and One Dot Product

The naive kernel assigns one output element to one thread, exactly the pattern our vecadd used, and its body is a dot product marching across global memory. Each thread reads one full row of the first matrix and one full column of the second, multiplies them pairwise, and accumulates in a register. The guard from earlier chapters stays in place for the smaller verification runs at n equal to 512, even though the benchmark sizes never trigger it.

We will now add the kernel to **kernels/src/lib.rs**:

```
#[kernel]
pub unsafe fn gemm_naive(a: &[f32], b: &[f32], c: *mut f32, n: usize) {
    let col = (thread::block_idx_x() * thread::block_dim_x() +
thread::thread_idx_x()) as usize;
    let row = (thread::block_idx_y() * thread::block_dim_y() +
thread::thread_idx_y()) as usize;
    if row < n && col < n {
        let mut sum = 0.0f32;
        for k in 0..n {
            sum += a[row * n + k] * b[k * n + col];
```

```
        }
        *c.add(row * n + col) = sum;
    }
}
```

The kernel deserves one admiring sentence before we condemn it, because this simplicity is why the naive form remains valuable. Every GEMM implementation we will ever debug gets verified against something shaped like this, since ten lines with no barriers, no tiles, and no cleverness leave very little room to be wrong. The professional pattern is to keep the naive version alive in the codebase as an oracle even after the fast version ships, and our benchmark does exactly that.

Why Cache cannot Save?

Not one line of the code is wrong, and everything about its memory behavior is. Each thread streams two n length vectors from global memory, the threads beside it reread almost the same data with nobody sharing, and the kernel achieves 0.62 teraflops on our reference machine, roughly two percent of peak. The GPU spent the run starved rather than busy. For contrast, the same algorithm compiled from CUDA C++ lands at 0.63, a rounding difference that already hints at the scoreboard's conclusion, since two compilers given the same starved memory pattern can only tie.

A fair question is why the L2 cache does not rescue the naive kernel, since neighboring threads read overlapping rows. It helps, and it is nowhere near enough, because a 4096 squared matrix occupies 64 megabytes against a few megabytes of cache, so rows are evicted long before their reuse arrives. A cache rewards temporal locality that fits, and the reuse window of GEMM at this size only fits when we cut it into tiles ourselves. The shared memory version is exactly that cut, performed with intent instead of hope.

Tiled Kernel

Marching Tiles through Shared Memory

The tiled approach attacks the rereads directly. The output is cut into 32 by 32 tiles, one per block, and the inputs march through shared memory one tile pair at a time, with each thread loading exactly one element of each tile per step. After the barrier, all one thousand twenty-four threads compute against data that now lives tens of cycles away instead of hundreds, and every loaded element is reused thirty-two times. The choreography is an earlier chapter's write, synchronize, read discipline applied twice per loop iteration, and the march appears in Fig 9.2:

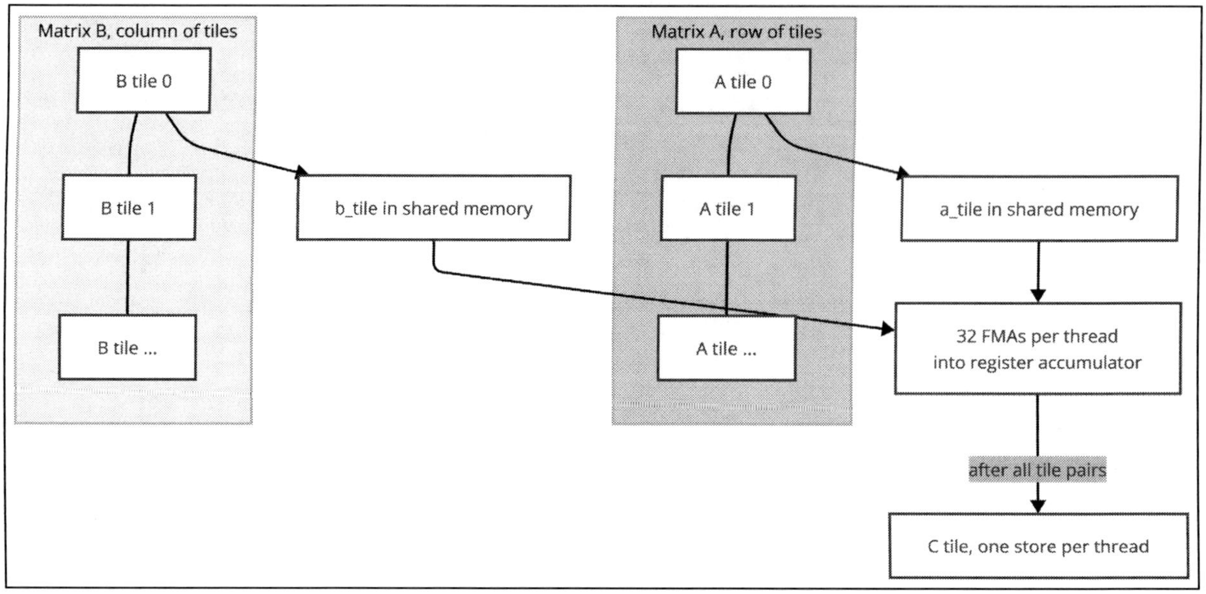

Fig 9.2: One Output Tile Consuming Tile Pairs

We will then add the tiled kernel beside the naive one:

```
#[kernel]
pub unsafe fn gemm_tiled(a: &[f32], b: &[f32], c: *mut f32, n: usize) {
    let a_tile = shared_array![f32; TILE * TILE];
    let b_tile = shared_array![f32; TILE * TILE];

    let tx = thread::thread_idx_x() as usize;
    let ty = thread::thread_idx_y() as usize;
    let row = thread::block_idx_y() as usize * TILE + ty;
    let col = thread::block_idx_x() as usize * TILE + tx;

    let mut sum = 0.0f32;
    for t in 0..(n / TILE) {
        // Phase 1: each thread loads one element of each tile, coalesced.
        (*a_tile)[ty * TILE + tx] = a[row * n + t * TILE + tx];
        (*b_tile)[ty * TILE + tx] = b[(t * TILE + ty) * n + col];
        thread::sync_threads();
```

```
        // Phase 2: 32 fused multiply-adds from shared memory.
        for k in 0..TILE {
            sum += (*a_tile)[ty * TILE + k] * (*b_tile)[k * TILE + tx];
        }
        thread::sync_threads();
    }
    *c.add(row * n + col) = sum;
}
```

Reading Kernel and Its Payoff

A reading pass over the kernel connects it to everything we have practiced. The two shared tiles fill with one coalesced load per thread, the row index rides the slow thread coordinate and the column rides the fast one, exactly an earlier chapter orientation. The first barrier protects the fills, the inner loop performs thirty-two fused multiply adds from shared memory, and the second barrier protects the tiles from the next iteration's fills. The accumulator never leaves its register until the single final store, which is the entire secret of the intensity gain.

A bookkeeping view makes the gain quantitative before the stopwatch confirms it. In the naive kernel, each of the two n cubed operations required a fresh global load, while here every element fetched from global memory serves thirty-two multiply adds, so the traffic to the warehouse falls by a factor of the tile width. Our roofline position slides rightward by exactly that factor, which carries the kernel off the bandwidth slope and onto ground where the arithmetic units finally set the pace.

The payoff is large and the numbers say precisely how large. Our tiled kernel reaches 4.3 teraflops, a sevenfold improvement over naive from the same arithmetic in a different order, and its CUDA C++ twin reaches 4.4. We should note that both versions assume the dimension divides by the tile width, an assumption our benchmark honors and a production guard would generalize. The remaining gap to the ceiling is real, and closing it involves register blocking, double buffering, and vectorized loads, the professional depths we acknowledge and deliberately do not enter.

The restraint deserves its reason, because the next rungs on this ladder change character rather than merely difficulty. Below tiling, each further teraflop costs disproportionately more code, couples the kernel to one architecture's register file and instruction mix, and produces exactly the software that libraries exist to maintain on our behalf. Our sevenfold gain came from a portable idea explained in one figure, while the next fourfold belongs to specialists with schematics, and knowing where that line falls is itself the lesson.

Library Ceiling

Calling cuBLAS through Raw Bindings

With cuBLAS, NVIDIA ships its dense linear algebra library, tuned per architecture by engineers with access to the hardware schematics, and calling it from Rust takes a handle, a function, and respect for one convention. The library speaks column major, the Fortran heritage every BLAS share, while our buffers are row major, and the standard trick computes our product by swapping the operand order, a wrinkle chapter 10 unpacks properly. The call below goes through the raw cublas-sys bindings, and chapter 10 will wrap this exact pattern safely.

So here, we will add the library call to **gemm_bench** as below:

```
use cublas_sys::*;

let mut handle: cublasHandle_t = std::ptr::null_mut();
let (alpha, beta) = (1.0f32, 0.0f32);

// SAFETY: handle is created before use and destroyed after; the
// device pointers outlive the call; dimensions match the buffers.
unsafe {
    cublasCreate_v2(&mut handle);

    // Row-major trick: compute C^T = B^T * A^T by swapping operands.
    cublasSgemm_v2(
        handle,
        cublasOperation_t::CUBLAS_OP_N,
        cublasOperation_t::CUBLAS_OP_N,
        n as i32, n as i32, n as i32,
        &alpha,
        d_b.as_device_ptr().as_raw() as *const f32, n as i32,
        d_a.as_device_ptr().as_raw() as *const f32, n as i32,
        &beta,
        d_c.as_device_ptr().as_raw() as *mut f32, n as i32,
    );

    cublasDestroy_v2(handle);
}
```

The handle deserves attention because it is our first stateful library object. A cublasCreate call builds it once, it carries workspace and stream binding for every subsequent call, and cublasDestroy releases it, a lifecycle begging for the Drop treatment that chapter 10 gives it. The Sgemm signature then takes the operation flags, the three dimensions, the scaling factors alpha and beta, and three device pointers with their leading dimensions. Every argument is a plain number or pointer, which is exactly why the raw call is unsafe and wrappable.

The operand swap in the comment rewards thirty seconds of thought rather than blind trust. Because a row major matrix read as column major is its own transpose, asking the library for B times A in its convention delivers the transpose of our desired product, laid out in memory exactly as we store results, so no data movement or transpose kernel is ever needed. The trick costs nothing at run time, and we will let chapter 10 derive it carefully once, so that every later call site can simply cite it.

Two Thirds of Peak

The ceiling lands at 19.8 teraflops on our machine, roughly two thirds of theoretical peak and four and a half times our tiled kernel. The comparison is humbling and clarifying at once, because a morning of honest work brought us within five percent of hand written CUDA C++, while years of NVIDIA engineering sit between both of us and the library, and no reasonable project budget closes that distance from scratch. The professional conclusion writes itself, and it becomes the decision rule of chapter 10, namely write kernels for the shapes libraries do not serve, and call libraries for the shapes they do.

Even the missing third of peak tells an honest story worth hearing. The theoretical number assumes every cycle issues a fused multiply add with operands already in registers, a condition no real schedule sustains across sixteen thousand blocks, barriers, and memory traffic. The engineers who build such libraries regard two thirds of FP32 peak at this size as excellent, and the figure climbs further with tensor cores and mixed precision, features cuBLAS exploits on newer architectures and our FP32 protocol deliberately leaves aside for comparability.

Scoreboard

Six Bars, Two Ties

The scoreboard collects the chapter and settles the question an earlier chapter posed. The hand written kernels tie across languages, with Rust and CUDA C++ separated by rounding error at both algorithm levels, which confirms that the codegen pipelines from Chapters 4 and 5 emit competitive PTX for regular kernels. The library rows tie as well, since Rust through cublas-sys and Python through CuPy both spend their time inside the identical binary. All six bars appear in Fig 9.3:

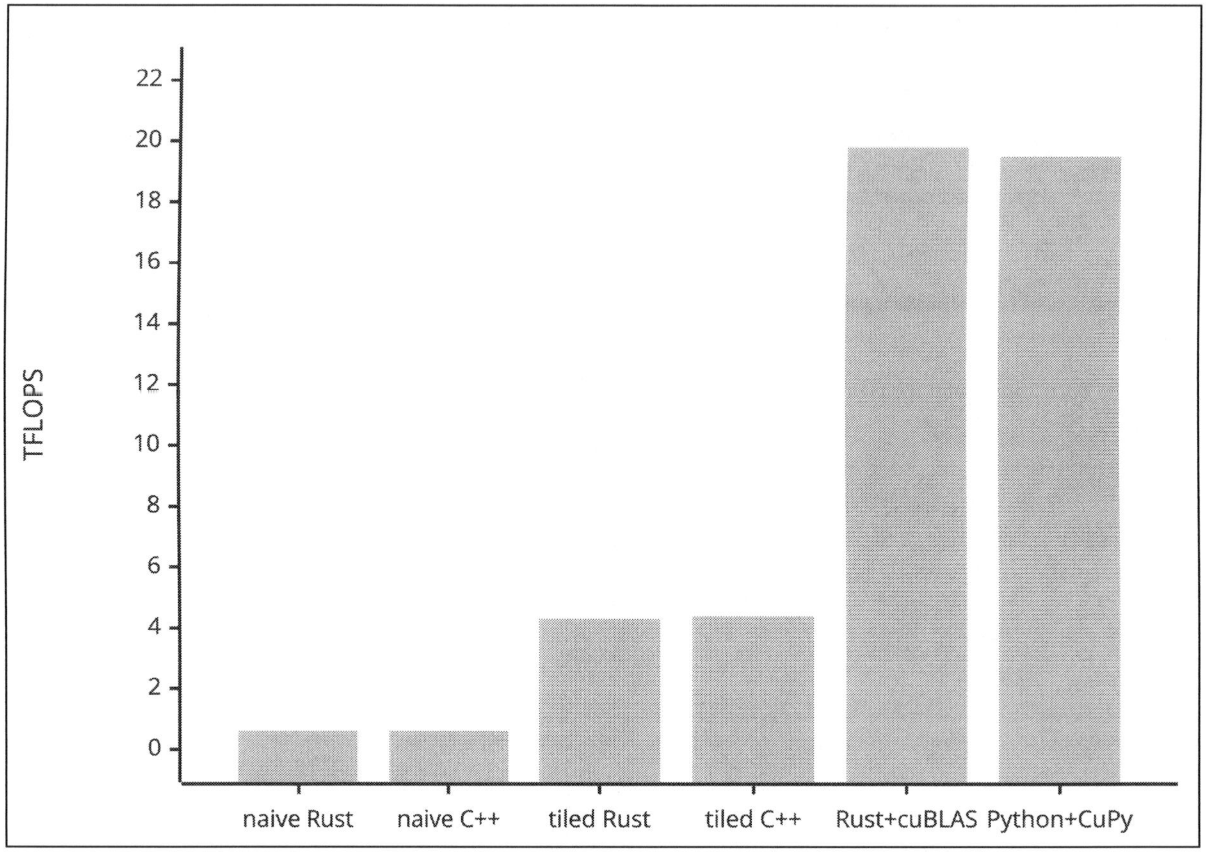

Fig 9.3: Scoreboard (n = 4096)

We will now run **`cargo run -p gemm_bench`**, and it reproduces the whole table:

```
gemm_naive   (Rust):     0.62 TFLOPS   verified vs CPU @512, vs cuBLAS @4096
gemm_naive   (C++):      0.63 TFLOPS
gemm_tiled   (Rust):     4.30 TFLOPS   verified
gemm_tiled   (C++):      4.41 TFLOPS
cuBLAS via Rust:        19.80 TFLOPS   reference result
cuBLAS via CuPy:        19.52 TFLOPS
```

The C++ twins deserve a sentence of methodology, because fair comparison is easy to fumble. We compile both twins with **`nvcc`** at O3 for the native architecture, implement line for line the same algorithms with the same tile width and the same launch shapes, and run them under the identical event timing harness over the identical data buffers. We are comparing code generation, not cleverness. Any reordering trick granted to one side would poison the conclusion, and the repository layout keeps the pairs adjacent so a suspicious eye can diff them in seconds.

Footnotes for Table

We should place two honest footnotes under the scoreboard. First, Python's parity holds because CuPy dispatches straight to cuBLAS, and it would hold for PyTorch equally, so nothing here embarrasses Python for library shaped work, exactly as an earlier chapter predicted, and the front desk from our opening chapter remains a perfectly good place to stand when the workload fits it. Second, the differences appear at the edges, since Python pays interpreter overhead per call, which matters for small matrices and tight loops, and Rust pays nothing there. At n equal to 256 the same benchmark shows Rust plus cuBLAS ahead by a third, a gap that is all call overhead and no arithmetic.

The full scoreboard run finishes in under a minute, and a fresh rerun is the point of shipping it as a workspace member. The numbers in a book age the moment the next driver releases, so the table above records one machine on one day, and the relationships between rows are the durable content. On any Ampere or newer card, we expect the same ordering, similar ratios between naive, tiled, and library, and the same language ties, and a run that breaks the pattern is a finding worth chasing rather than a disappointment.

A final word belongs to the audience this scoreboard quietly addresses, namely the colleague who asks why the team should consider Rust at all when C++ owns GPU computing and Python owns its users. The table answers without rhetoric, since it shows Rust matching C++ where code is written and matching Python where libraries are called, while bringing the ownership and error handling advantages the earlier chapters demonstrated. Whether those advantages justify a migration is a judgment call for each team, and now it is at least a call made on measurements.

Our workspace now delivers real math at honest speeds. We watched one algorithm span a thirtyfold performance range purely on memory choreography, confirmed that Rust kernels match their C++ twins, and located the library ceiling that no weekend kernel approaches. The **`gemm_bench`** member preserves the whole experiment for any machine to rerun, verification gates and fair twins included, so the scoreboard remains a living instrument rather than a printed claim. In chapter 10, we stop treating cuBLAS as a single mysterious call and learn to wrap the NVIDIA libraries properly, because production Rust mixes custom kernels with library calls, and the seam between them deserves the same engineering care we have spent on everything else.

CHAPTER 10
BORROWING NVIDIA's MUSCLE

In this chapter, we learn to borrow. Over the years, NVIDIA has packaged decades of engineering as libraries, and chapter 9 showed the ceiling they set, so a professional Rust GPU program mixes custom kernels with library calls and treats the seam between them as a design surface. We will establish a working rule for when to write and when to call, learn the conventions that make cuBLAS cooperate with row major Rust, and add random number generation to our toolkit from both the host side and the device side.

The engineering heart of the chapter is wrapper design, because raw bindings are where C's sharp edges reenter a Rust program. We will build a small safe wrapper over cuBLAS with handles that clean up, status codes that become errors, and methods that accept our typed buffers, and the pattern generalizes to any C library we ever need. The project then earns its keep in finance, since a Monte Carlo option pricer combines device randomness, a custom payoff kernel, and a library reduction, and validates against a closed formula. A little finance vocabulary arrives with it, and we will define each term in one plain sentence when it appears, so no prior exposure to markets is assumed anywhere in the chapter.

When to Write and When to Call?

Decision in Order

The decision rule from chapter 9 deserves a fuller statement, because it guides real budgets. We call a library when our shape matches its shape, since nobody outruns cuBLAS on square GEMM from a standing start, and we write a kernel when the operation is fused, unusual, or small enough that call overhead dominates. The middle ground is fusion, where a custom kernel merge steps a library would perform separately and saves round trips through global memory. These tests fold into the order we actually apply them in Fig 10.1:

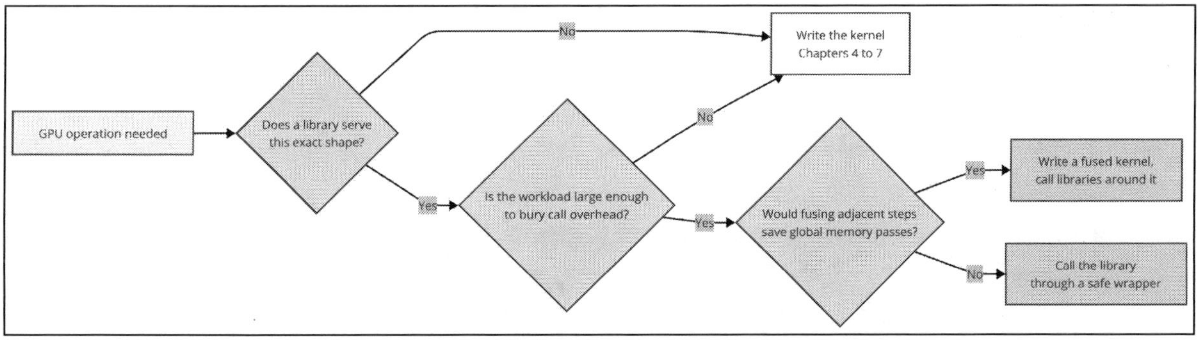

Fig 10.1: Write-or-Call Decision

The overhead side of the rule has numbers from our own scoreboard. A library call costs microseconds of launch and dispatch, which vanishes under the milliseconds of a 4096 GEMM and dominates the microseconds of a 128 GEMM, and the small matrix footnote of chapter 9 measured exactly that inversion. The fusion case has numbers too, since every avoided round trip through global memory saves both a kernel launch and a full pass of bandwidth. The rule is therefore not taste but arithmetic, and it changes verdicts as sizes change.

Library Shelf

The library shelf is broader than this book can cover, and a map helps. Beside cuBLAS sit cuFFT for transforms, cuRAND for randomness, cuSPARSE for sparse matrices, and cuDNN for deep learning primitives, all documented at docs.nvidia.com. The Rust coverage varies honestly, with thin sys crates existing for most, the Rust-CUDA project shipping curand and cudnn wrappers in varying states of polish, and nothing stopping us from binding any C API ourselves, which is precisely the skill this chapter installs. Our rule is to prefer a maintained wrapper and to wrap thinly when none exists.

A word on trust rounds out the map, because borrowed muscle still deserves inspection. Whenever we weigh a wrapper crate, we will glance at three things, namely its recency of maintenance, whether its version tracks the toolkit versions we run, and whether its API exposes Results or panics. A crate that panics on library errors undoes the vocabulary we have built since an earlier chapter, and in that case a thin wrapper of our own, built from the template this chapter teaches, is often the calmer choice.

Linear Algebra with cuBLAS

Column Major and Row Major

The column major convention is the one genuine friction in calling BLAS from Rust. A BLAS routine believes matrices are stored column after column, the Fortran way, while our slices store row after row, and no flag in the classic Sgemm interface simply says row major. A row major buffer read with column major eyes produces the transpose, and that observation is the whole escape.

The same sixteen numbers wear both interpretations in Fig 10.2:

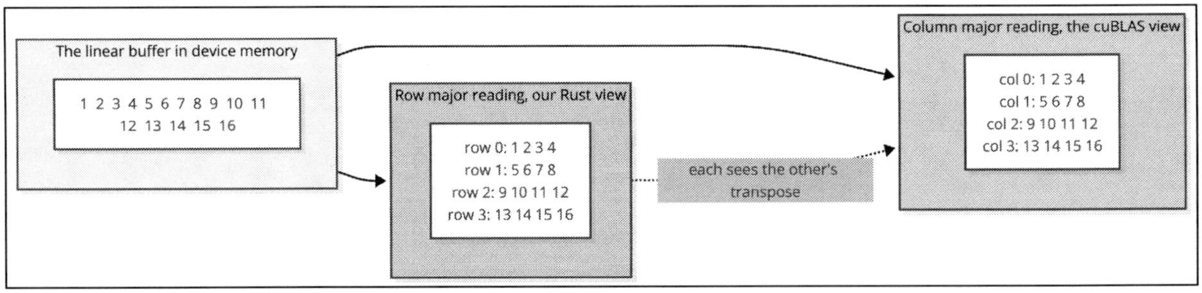

Fig 10.2: One Buffer, Two Interpretations

The swap trick follows in one line of algebra. A transposition reverses a product, so C transpose equals B transpose times A transpose, and since column major eyes see each of our row major buffers as its transpose, a request to cuBLAS for B times A in its world writes exactly our C in ours. The leading dimension arguments tell the library the stride between consecutive columns, which for our dense square case is simply n. The raw call in chapter 9 already used both facts, and our wrapper will hide them behind a method named for what it does.

Two Minute Convention Test

A two-minute test protects us from convention bugs forever. Whenever a BLAS integration is new to us, we will multiply two small deliberately asymmetric matrices, ones whose product differs visibly from the product of their transposes, and compare against a CPU loop. A square symmetric test can pass with the convention wrong, which is how these bugs survive review. Our **gemm_bench** member carries exactly this test from chapter 9 onward, and it takes microseconds to run beside everything else.

The habit generalizes beyond BLAS to every convention boundary a program crosses. When any two systems disagree about layout, endianness, units, or index origin, the professional move is a tiny test with deliberately asymmetric data pinned permanently into the build, because convention bugs produce plausible numbers rather than crashes. We would rather learn about a flipped matrix from a failing test named after the convention than from a quarter of confusing model results downstream.

Random Numbers on Device

We can take two roads to carry randomness onto the GPU. The host road uses cuRAND's generator API, where curandCreateGenerator and curandGenerateUniform fill a device buffer with millions of samples in one call, and it suits programs that consume randomness as input data. The device road generates inside the kernel, one generator per thread, and it suits simulations where each thread walks its own random path, because shipping paths from a buffer would cost more bandwidth than computing them. Our pricer takes the device road, and the **gpu_rand** crate from the Rust-CUDA project paves it.

Host Road with cuRAND

The host road deserves its own five lines, because many programs need nothing more:

```
let mut gen: curandGenerator_t = std::ptr::null_mut();
unsafe {
    curandCreateGenerator(&mut gen, CURAND_RNG_PSEUDO_XORWOW);
    curandSetPseudoRandomGeneratorSeed(gen, 42);
    curandGenerateUniform(gen, d_buf.as_device_ptr().as_raw() as *mut f32, 
n);
    curandDestroyGenerator(gen);
```

```
}
```

The generator object fills any device buffer with uniforms or normals at tens of gigasamples per second, the seed call makes runs reproducible, and the whole surface begs for the same wrapper treatment we are about to give cuBLAS, with create checked, destroy in Drop, and generate accepting a typed buffer. The five raw calls above carry the same C dangers we have named all chapter, an unchecked status, a leak on early return, and a pointer cast the compiler must take on faith. We leave that wrapper as the chapter's exercise, since it repeats our template with different nouns, and a finished version makes a satisfying first contribution for anyone extending the workspace beyond this book. The fixed seed of 42 in the listing is the reproducibility habit every simulation team swears by, because a bug that appears under one seed must be chased under that same seed.

Device Road with 'gpu_rand'

The **`gpu_rand`** crate implements the xoroshiro generator family, small fast generators with solid statistical properties that Blackman and Vigna analyze in Scrambled Linear Pseudorandom Number Generators in ACM TOMS. Each thread seeds its own generator from a base seed plus its global index, which makes runs reproducible and threads decorrelated enough for our purposes. One honest caveat belongs here, since per thread seeding is not a cryptographic practice and heavy production simulations use sequence splitting instead, a refinement the crate documentation and the cuRAND manual both describe.

The choice between the two roads follows the bandwidth reasoning of an earlier chapter rather than any preference about APIs. A buffer of pregenerated randoms is data that must cross or occupy global memory, while a per thread generator is a few registers of state that produce values exactly where they are consumed. For our pricer, each path needs only two draws, so generation in registers is clearly cheaper than a sixteen million element buffer of draws, and the same accounting will point the other way for algorithms that reuse one random table many times.

Designing Safe Wrappers

Anatomy in Layers

A safe wrapper is a thin crate with a strict anatomy, and every layer has one job. At the bottom sits the sys crate, machine generated declarations of the C functions, all unsafe. Above it, our wrapper owns the library handle in a newtype, converts every status code into a Rust error enum, exposes methods that accept typed device buffers rather than raw pointers, and implements Drop so teardown cannot be forgotten. The application on top never sees a pointer, and that sentence is the entire specification of success for this section. The layers stack in Fig 10.3:

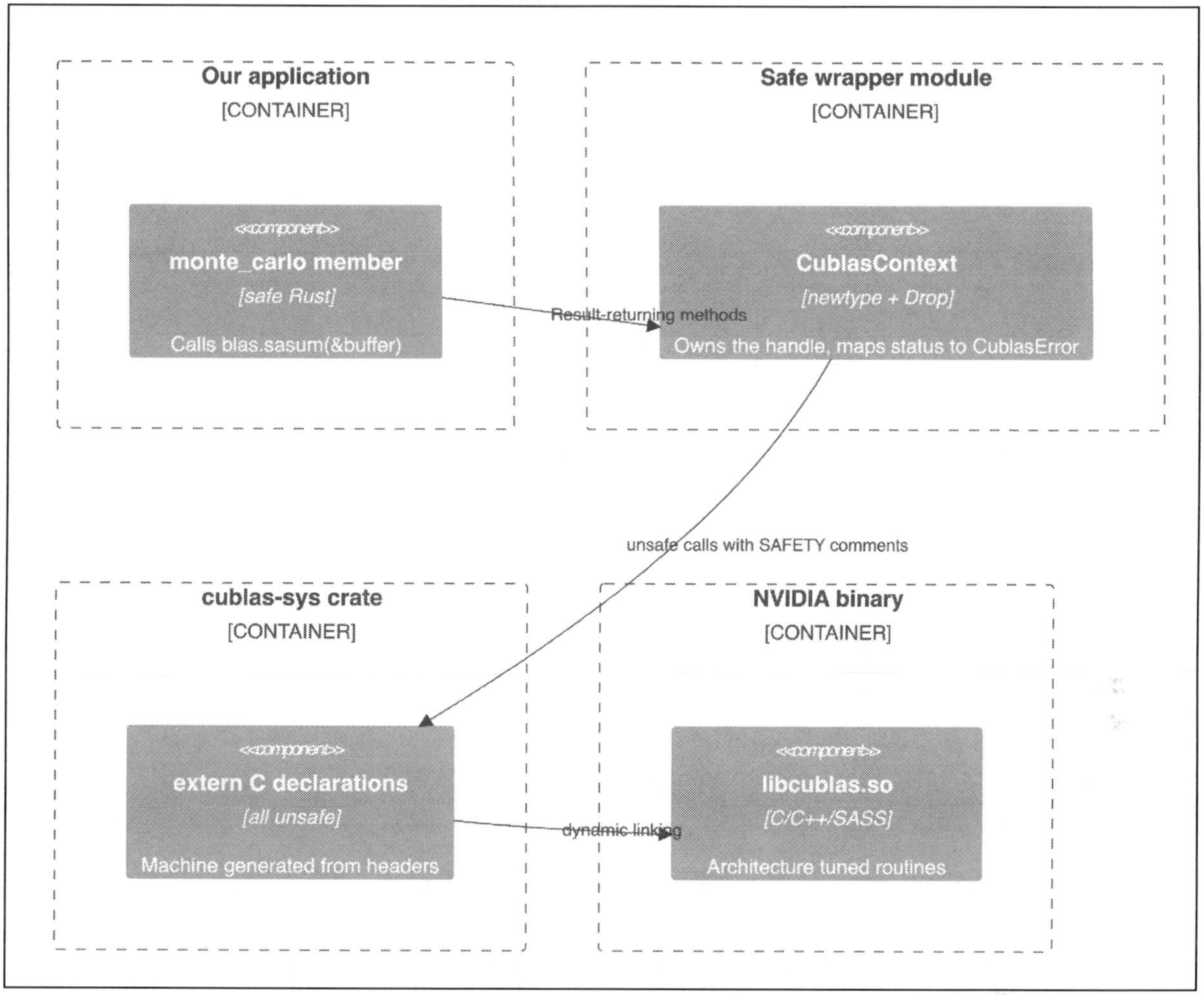

Fig 10.3: Wrapper Anatomy

The discipline of the diagram lies in what never crosses its boundaries. A raw pointer exists below the wrapper line and a **`Result`** exists above it, and no layer leaks its vocabulary upward, so the application code stays reviewable by teammates who have never read a CUDA header. This is the same layering that operating systems and databases practice internally, applied at the scale of a single module, and the payoff arrives every time a new person joins the codebase and reads the top layer first.

Five Moves Applied to cuBLAS

The template has five moves, and they apply to any C library. First, we wrap the handle in a struct with a private field. Second, we make the constructor return a **`Result`** by checking the create call's status. Third, we mirror the status enum as a Rust error type with a conversion. Fourth, we write one method per operation we actually use, and we let each accept references to our buffer types, translate to pointers internally, and carry its SAFETY comment. Fifth, we implement **Drop** with the destroy call. The listing runs longer than our usual excerpts because a wrapper deserves seeing whole at least once.

We will now apply all five to cuBLAS in a new module as below:

```
use cublas_sys::*;
use cust::memory::DeviceBuffer;

#[derive(Debug)]
pub enum CublasError {
    NotInitialized,
    AllocFailed,
    InvalidValue,
    ExecutionFailed,
    Other(u32),
}

fn check(status: cublasStatus_t) -> Result<(), CublasError> {
    use cublasStatus_t::*;
    match status {
        CUBLAS_STATUS_SUCCESS => Ok(()),
        CUBLAS_STATUS_NOT_INITIALIZED => Err(CublasError::NotInitialized),
        CUBLAS_STATUS_ALLOC_FAILED => Err(CublasError::AllocFailed),
        CUBLAS_STATUS_INVALID_VALUE => Err(CublasError::InvalidValue),
        CUBLAS_STATUS_EXECUTION_FAILED =>
Err(CublasError::ExecutionFailed),
        other => Err(CublasError::Other(other as u32)),
    }
}

pub struct CublasContext {
    handle: cublasHandle_t,
}
```

```
impl CublasContext {
    pub fn new() -> Result<Self, CublasError> {
        let mut handle = std::ptr::null_mut();
        // SAFETY: the pointer is valid for the write; status is checked.
        check(unsafe { cublasCreate_v2(&mut handle) })?;
        Ok(Self { handle })
    }

    /// Sum of absolute values of a device buffer.
    pub fn sasum(&self, x: &DeviceBuffer<f32>) -> Result<f32, CublasError>
{
        let mut result = 0.0f32;
        // SAFETY: x outlives the call; the length matches the buffer.
        check(unsafe {
            cublasSasum_v2(
                self.handle,
                x.len() as i32,
                x.as_device_ptr().as_raw() as *const f32,
                1,
                &mut result,
            )
        })?;
        Ok(result)
    }
}

impl Drop for CublasContext {
    fn drop(&mut self) {
        // SAFETY: the handle was created in new() and never destroyed
elsewhere.
        unsafe {
            cublasDestroy_v2(self.handle);
        }
    }
```

```
}
```

We should emphasize two design points in the wrapper. The error enum means a failed library call now travels the same question mark road as every CUDA error since an earlier chapter, and nothing library shaped can fail silently anymore. And the missing Sync implementation is deliberate honesty, because a cuBLAS handle is not safe for simultaneous use from multiple threads, so we let Rust's auto traits forbid exactly what the library documentation warns against. A C++ wrapper states such rules in comments, while ours states them in the type system.

The thinness of the wrapper is a virtue worth defending against the urge to improve it. We expose only **sasum** today because only the pricer needs it, and each future project adds the one or two methods it requires, so the wrapper grows along the grain of actual use rather than toward imagined completeness. A wrapper that mirrors an entire library becomes a maintenance project of its own, while ours stays small enough to review over coffee, and reviewability was the entire reason we built it.

Monte Carlo Option Pricing

Why Simulate Solved Problem?

Our project prices a European call option, the hello world of computational finance with the rare virtue of a closed form referee. Under the Black Scholes model, the option's value has an exact formula, while the Monte Carlo method estimates the same value by simulation, with millions of terminal prices averaged into a discounted expectation under the law of large numbers. With spot 100, strike 100, rate 0.05, volatility 0.2, and one year, the formula says 10.4506, and our estimator must approach that number as samples grow, which is a sharper test than any of our previous verifications.

A reader who has never met options need not worry, since the contract fits in three sentences. A European call grants the right, without obligation, to buy an asset at a fixed strike price on a fixed future date, so its payoff is the amount by which the final price exceeds the strike, or nothing. Its fair value today is the average of those payoffs over the asset's possible futures, discounted for interest. All the rest of this project is machinery for computing that average sixteen million futures at a time.

A fair question is why anyone simulates what a formula already solves. The formula exists only for the simplest contracts, and the moment a payoff depends on the path, the average price, or several correlated assets, closed forms vanish while the simulation barely changes shape. So practitioners validate their Monte Carlo machinery on the solvable case, exactly as we do, and then point the same machinery at the unsolvable ones. Our pricer is the validation half of that workflow, and its structure is the production half.

One Thread and One Path

The kernel gives each thread one complete simulation. A thread seeds its generator, draws two uniforms, converts them to a standard normal with the Box Muller transform, advances the price under geometric Brownian motion in one analytic step, and writes its discounted payoff. No thread ever waits on another, no shared memory appears, and the whole simulation is embarrassingly parallel, the technical term for the best kind of luck.

We will now add the kernel to **kernels/src/lib.rs**:

```
use gpu_rand::DefaultRand;
use rand_core::{RngCore, SeedableRng};

#[kernel]
pub unsafe fn price_paths(
    seed: u64,
    s0: f32,
    k: f32,
    r: f32,
    sigma: f32,
    t: f32,
    payoffs: *mut f32,
    n: usize,
) {
    let i = thread::index_1d() as usize;
    if i < n {
        let mut rng = DefaultRand::seed_from_u64(seed + i as u64);

        // Two uniforms in (0, 1], then Box-Muller to a standard normal.
        let u1 = ((rng.next_u32() >> 8) as f32 / 16_777_216.0).max(1e-7);
        let u2 = (rng.next_u32() >> 8) as f32 / 16_777_216.0;
        let z = (-2.0 * u1.ln()).sqrt() * (2.0 * core::f32::consts::PI *
u2).cos();

        // Terminal price under geometric Brownian motion, one exact step.
        let st = s0 * ((r - 0.5 * sigma * sigma) * t + sigma * t.sqrt() *
z).exp();
```

```
        let payoff = (st - k).max(0.0);
        *payoffs.add(i) = (-r * t).exp() * payoff;
    }
}
```

The mathematics compresses pleasantly into Rust. The Box Muller transform turns two uniform draws into one normal draw with a logarithm, a square root, and a cosine, all routed to GPU intrinsics by **cuda_std**. The terminal price uses the exact solution of geometric Brownian motion, so no time stepping loop is needed for a European payoff. And our scalar parameters ride to the device as kernel arguments, which the hardware serves from a constant memory bank, so they enjoy the broadcast efficiency an earlier chapter promised without any ceremony from us.

Assembling and Converging

The host assembles the pipeline from parts we own. It launches the kernel over sixteen million threads, asks our wrapper's sasum method for the sum of payoffs, which equals the plain sum because payoffs are never negative, and divides by the sample size on the CPU, since one division deserves no kernel. We could equally have reused the reduction kernel of an earlier chapter for the sum, and the library call wins here on the chapter 10 rule itself, namely that a served shape at sufficient size belongs to the library. The run repeats at one million samples to show the error shrinking with the square root law.

We will then add the pricing flow to a new member named **monte_carlo**:

```
let blas = CublasContext::new()?;
let prices = module.get_function("price_paths")?;

for &n in &[1_000_000usize, 16_000_000] {
    let mut d_payoffs = DeviceBuffer::<f32>::zeroed(n)?;
    let grid = (n as u32).div_ceil(256);

    unsafe {
        launch!(prices<<<grid, 256, 0, stream>>>(
            42u64,
            100.0f32, 100.0f32, 0.05f32, 0.2f32, 1.0f32,
            d_payoffs.as_device_ptr(),
            n
        ))?;
    }
```

```
    stream.synchronize()?;

    let sum = blas.sasum(&d_payoffs)?;
    println!("n = {:>9}: price = {:.4}", n, sum / n as f32);
}
println!("Black-Scholes closed form: 10.4506");
```

The pricer converges on our reference machine exactly as ordered:

```
n =    1000000: price = 10.4419
n =   16000000: price = 10.4482
Black-Scholes closed form: 10.4506
```

The estimates bracket the formula exactly as theory predicts. At one million samples the estimate sits within about a cent of 10.4506, at sixteen million within a quarter of a cent, and the error falls by the expected factor of four for the sixteenfold sample increase. The full pipeline that produced them appears in Fig 10.4. Every stage is a skill from a previous chapter, and the only new ingredient today was the seam engineering that let a library reduction sit naturally beside a custom kernel:

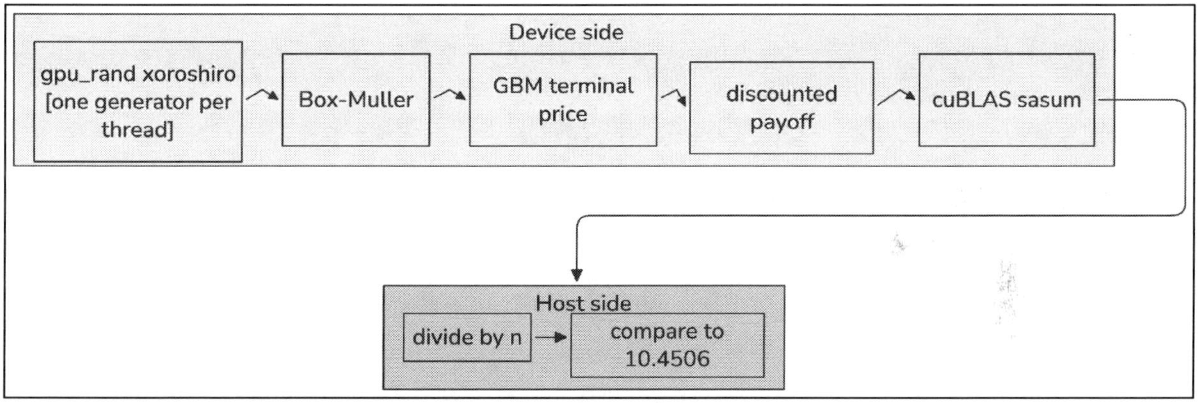

Fig 10.4: Monte Carlo Pricing Pipeline

The speed lands where chapter 9 taught us to expect it. All sixteen million simulations complete in under four milliseconds of device time, since each thread performs a few dozen arithmetic operations on values that never leave registers, and the single payoff buffer is the only global memory traffic. The same estimate takes our reference CPU several seconds single threaded, a gap that grows with path dependent contracts. The result is a workload where the GPU's advantage is honest and enormous at once, unlike the vecadd humility of an earlier chapter.

The convergence table also rehearses a conversation every quantitative team eventually has, namely how many samples a result deserves. Because the error shrinks with the square root of the sample count, each extra digit of precision costs a hundredfold more compute, and the four-millisecond price of sixteen million paths tells us instantly what any target accuracy will cost in device time. We now own the instrument that turns that budgeting question into arithmetic, which is worth more than the price it just computed.

The borrowing habit is now part of our practice. We can decide write versus call on technical grounds, speak column major without translation errors, generate randomness on whichever side of the bus the algorithm prefers, and wrap any C library so that its failures become Results and its cleanup becomes Drop. The pricer validated against an exact formula, which is the strongest referee this book has used, and the seam between our kernel and the library call proved invisible in the timings, which is what well engineered borrowing should look like. In chapter 11, everything converges, because the capstone pipeline will batch real inference through custom kernels, library calls, and async streams at once, and every seam it crosses will be one this chapter taught us to engineer. The wrapper we built today returns there with two new methods, which is exactly how thin wrappers are supposed to grow, one proven need at a time rather than one imagined feature at a time.

CHAPTER 11
SHIPPING COMPLETE GPU APPLICATION

In this chapter, everything we own goes to work at once. The capstone builds a batched inference pipeline for a small neural network, the kind of workload that pays GPU bills in production, and it uses no skill we have not already practiced. The GEMM calls come from an earlier chapter and the wrapper from chapter 10, the fused activation kernel applies earlier chapter patterns under the chapter 10 fusion rule, the streams and pinned ring come from Chapters 6 and 8, and the verification habit comes from everywhere.

Our subject is a multilayer perceptron with three dense layers, and inference means pushing batches of inputs through matrix multiplies and activations to produce a class prediction per sample. The cuda-oxide book builds its flagship project around exactly this shape, and we will follow its architecture while implementing on our dependable toolchain, and then sketch the async graph version beside it. As the chapter closes, we will measure throughput against a serial baseline and against Python with CuPy, and the numbers will summarize the book's whole argument.

Batched MLP Inference Pipeline

Modest Network and Real Workload

The network is deliberately modest, with an input of 784 features, hidden layers of 256 and 128 units, and 10 outputs, the classic shape of a digit classifier. The workload processes 65,536 samples as 64 batches of 1,024, which keeps each batch's input at 3.2 megabytes and its compute near half a gigaflop. The weights are synthetic, since our subject is the pipeline rather than accuracy, and correctness means agreement with a CPU forward pass within the floating-point tolerance an earlier chapter taught us to expect. A trained checkpoint would drop into the same buffers without changing a line of pipeline code, which is exactly the separation of concerns we want to demonstrate.

We will let two workspace members carry the chapter. The **`mlp_pipeline`** member holds the network definition, the batching layer, and both schedulers, while the familiar kernels crate gains the fused activation and the argmax. A small Python file rides in the repository beside them for the CuPy comparison, and any recent CuPy installation runs it without ceremony. All three share the verification data, which a fixed seed regenerates identically on every machine, so the three configurations we measure disagree about scheduling and language and about nothing else. A model this small keeps every effect we care about visible, since transfers, dispatch overhead, and scheduling all show up clearly when no single GEMM dominates the clock, while a large transformer would bury those lessons under compute. The pipeline patterns scale up unchanged, and the reader who swaps in bigger layers will find the architecture indifferent to the substitution.

Resident Weights and Flowing Batches

The architecture separates what stays resident from what flows. The three weight matrices and bias vectors upload once at startup and live on the device for the program's lifetime, roughly 900 kilobytes in total, a footprint so small beside the ten-gigabyte card that residency costs us nothing.

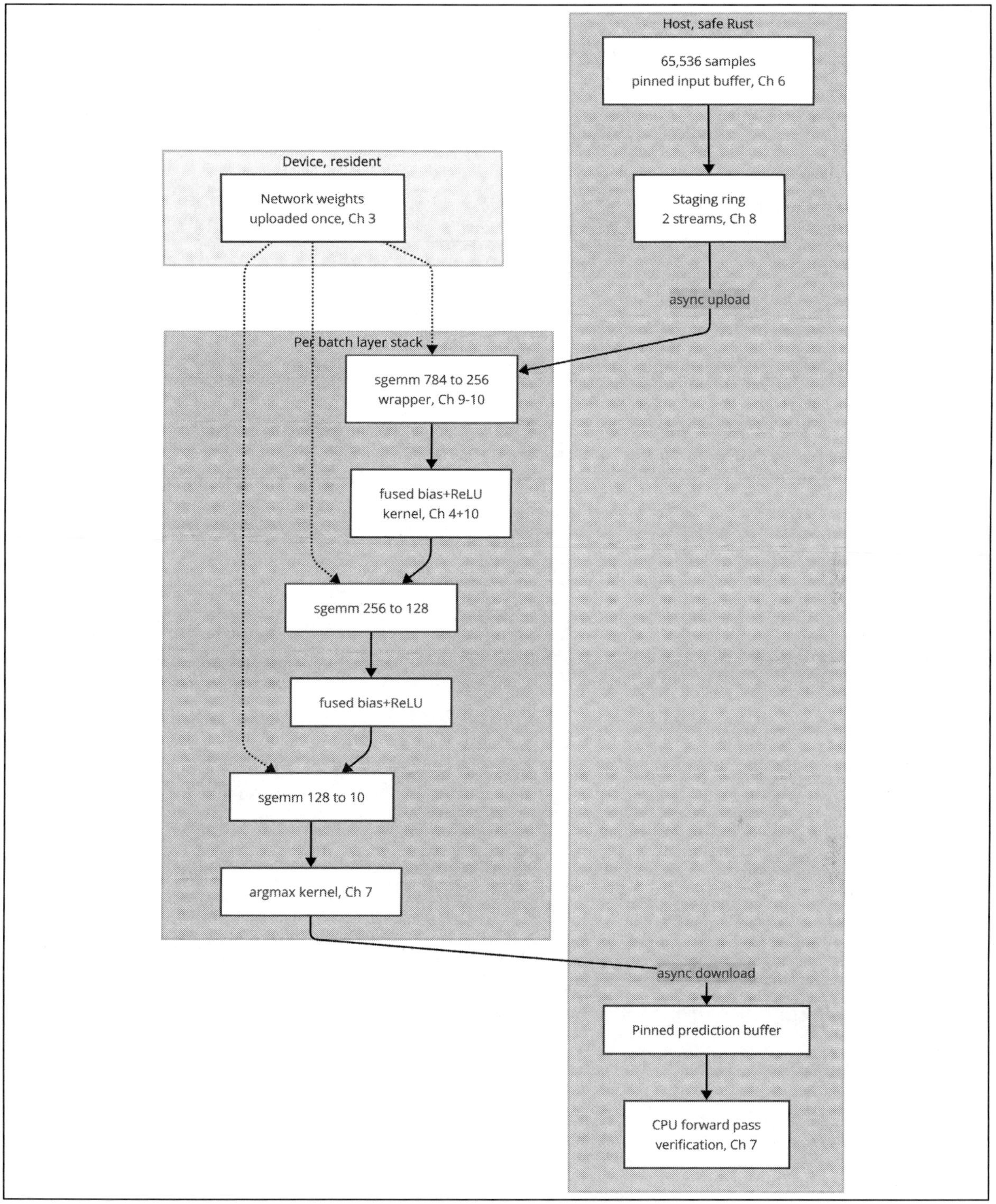

Fig 11.1: Capstone Architecture

The samples flow, batch by batch, through a pinned staging ring, across PCIe, through the layer stack, and back as one predicted class per sample, as shown in the above Fig 11.1. The layer stack applies chapter 10's decision rule three times and lands on a mixture. The matrix multiplies go to cuBLAS through our wrapper, since 1024 by 784 by 256 is squarely library territory. The bias addition and ReLU activation fuse into one custom kernel, because running them separately would drag the activations through global memory twice for two trivial operations. The final argmax is a small per row reduction from an earlier chapter's toolbox, written as a kernel because no single library call produces class indices from logits.

The mixture deserves a sentence of celebration before we descend into parts, because it is the destination the whole book has been walking toward. No single chapter could have built this stack, and no piece of it is new today, which means the capstone is genuinely an exercise in composition rather than invention. When our own projects reach this stage, the feeling to expect is mild anticlimax, and that feeling is the evidence of skills that have settled into habit.

Data Loading and Batching

Pinned Buffers and Staging Ring

The batching layer owns memory strategy, and pinned allocation from an earlier chapter is its foundation. The input samples live in one large **`LockedBuffer`**, sliced logically into batches, and the predictions return into a second pinned buffer, so every transfer in the program is eligible for the asynchronous path. The staging ring from an earlier chapter returns as well, with two device buffers per direction so one batch can upload while the previous one computes. None of this machinery is new, and that is the point of a capstone. The one adaptation worth noticing is scale, since an earlier chapter staged half a gigabyte of bytes while we stage 3.2-megabyte batches of floats, and the ring's design is indifferent to the difference, which is what a good abstraction owes us.

The resident side follows the structure of arrays advice from an earlier chapter at the scale of a network. Each layer's weight matrix uploads as one contiguous row major buffer, the biases as short vectors beside them, and a plain Rust struct named **`Network`** holds the device buffers with ownership doing the bookkeeping. When the program ends, Drop releases the lot in reverse declaration order, and no teardown code exists anywhere. A larger model would stream weights per layer, and the ring machinery we already own is exactly what that would reuse.

Choosing Batch Size

The batch size is a genuine tuning decision with a shape worth understanding. A small batch wastes the GPU, since a 1024 by 784 GEMM already sits near the small end of efficient library shapes, and it multiplies per batch overheads. A large batch raises latency, the time until the first predictions emerge, and it grows the staging footprint. Our 1,024 balances the two for this network, and the tools of chapter 12 can retune it per machine. A production system often exposes exactly this dial to operators, which tells us something about its importance.

A worked feel for the dial helps more than the abstract trade. At a batch of 128, each GEMM shrinks eightfold and the per batch overheads stay constant, so the overhead share of each turn grows sharply and throughput sags. At a batch of 8,192, the staging ring needs eight times the pinned memory, the first prediction waits eight times longer, and the throughput gain over 1,024 turns out to be modest because the GEMMs were already efficient. The sweet spot sits where the largest GEMM first reaches library efficiency, and that is a measurable property rather than folklore.

Compute Core

One Fused Kernel and Argmax

The compute core adds one kernel to our collection, and it is a deliberate fusion. The kernel receives the raw GEMM output, adds the bias for each column, applies the ReLU, and writes the result in place, one element per thread, with the bias index derived from the column position. The fusion follows the chapter 10 rule to the letter, since both fused steps are trivial alone and expensive to separate. A second small kernel converts the final logits into class predictions.

We will now add both to **kernels/src/lib.rs**:

```
#[kernel]
pub unsafe fn bias_relu(data: *mut f32, bias: &[f32], rows: usize, cols: usize) {
    let i = thread::index_1d() as usize;
    if i < rows * cols {
        let col = i % cols;
        let v = *data.add(i) + bias[col];
        *data.add(i) = v.max(0.0);
    }
}

#[kernel]
pub unsafe fn argmax_rows(logits: &[f32], preds: *mut u32, rows: usize, cols: usize) {
    let row = thread::index_1d() as usize;
    if row < rows {
        let mut best = 0usize;
```

```
        let mut best_v = logits[row * cols];
        for c in 1..cols {
            let v = logits[row * cols + c];
            if v > best_v {
                best_v = v;
                best = c;
            }
        }
        // One thread owns one row; ten columns need no cooperation.
        // A warp-per-row version pays off around a thousand classes.
        *preds.add(row) = best as u32;
    }
}
```

We will find both kernels reading like review, which after ten chapters is exactly the compliment, we hoped to pay ourselves. The fused kernel is an earlier chapter's element pattern with a two-dimensional twist, since each thread computes its column index to select the right bias, and the in-place write is legal for the familiar one thread one element reason. The argmax kernel gives each output row to one thread, a deliberately simple design that is fast enough because ten logits per row leave nothing worth parallelizing further. A warp per row version would shine at a thousand classes, and the comment in the code says so.

Scratch Memory and Forward Pass

A **Scratch** struct completes the memory picture, since every layer needs somewhere to write. The three activation buffers exist once per stream rather than once per batch, the same flat memory strategy as an earlier chapter's pipeline, and they never travel to the host at all. The intermediate activations are the pipeline's private business, and only the final predictions cross PCIe, which is why the download side of this pipeline moves kilobytes while the upload side moves megabytes. The asymmetry shapes the schedule, and the measurement section shows it. A pipeline that shipped its activations home between layers would triple its transfer budget for no benefit, and the discipline of keeping intermediates resident is among the most common wins available when porting a naive GPU port toward production shape.

The wrapper from chapter 10 grows two methods to serve the pipeline. A **set_stream** method binds the handle to whichever stream a batch rides, which is how library calls join our overlap choreography, and a **sgemm** method hides the swap trick from chapter 10 behind named row major arguments, so no call site in this chapter ever mentions a transpose again. With those in place, the whole layer stack becomes a short host function that any Rust programmer could read without GPU background, which is its own kind of milestone.

Ahead of the listing, we should notice what the function signature itself communicates. Every argument arrives as a reference with an explicit mutability, so a reviewer can see briefly that the weights are read only, the scratch buffers and predictions are written, and nothing is owned, retained, or leaked by the call itself. This is documentation the compiler enforces, and it is precisely the property that makes a six argument GPU function reviewable in a way its C counterpart, six raw pointers deep, never quite achieves.

We will then compose the forward pass as below:

```
fn forward_batch(
    blas: &CublasContext,
    stream: &Stream,
    x: &DeviceBuffer<f32>,          // 1024 x 784, this batch's input
    net: &Network,                  // resident weights and biases
    scratch: &mut Scratch,          // per-stream activation buffers
    preds: &mut DeviceBuffer<u32>,
) -> Result<(), Box<dyn Error>> {
    blas.set_stream(stream)?;

    blas.sgemm(x, &net.w1, &mut scratch.h1, 1024, 784, 256)?;
    launch_bias_relu(stream, &mut scratch.h1, &net.b1, 1024, 256)?;

    blas.sgemm(&scratch.h1, &net.w2, &mut scratch.h2, 1024, 256, 128)?;
    launch_bias_relu(stream, &mut scratch.h2, &net.b2, 1024, 128)?;

    blas.sgemm(&scratch.h2, &net.w3, &mut scratch.out, 1024, 128, 10)?;
    launch_argmax(stream, &scratch.out, preds, 1024, 10)?;

    Ok(())
}
```

Scheduling with Async Streams

Two Streams by Hand

The scheduler deals batches across two streams exactly as an earlier chapter rehearsed, with each batch's upload, eight device operations, and download all queued to one stream, and consecutive batches alternating streams. The per stream device buffers make the memory safety story identical to the stream pipelines, and the SAFETY comments transfer nearly verbatim. One addition earns attention, since the cuBLAS handle must follow the batch onto its stream, which is precisely what our **`set_stream`** method does at the top of each batch's turn.

The forgotten **`set_stream`** call is worth naming as the classic defect of mixed pipelines, because its symptom misleads so reliably. When the handle stays bound to the wrong stream, every result remains correct, since each batch's operations still execute in a valid order, and only the overlap silently disappears as library calls serialize behind a stranger's queue. The program passes every test and loses a third of its throughput, which is exactly the category of bug that only the profiling habits of chapter 12 catch.

Same Pipeline as Async Graph

The same pipeline has a striking second life in cuda-oxide's async model, and its book builds the flagship async MLP project this way. Each stage becomes a **`DeviceOperation`**, the layer stack composes with **`and_then`**, the weights ride beside data with **`zip!`** and **`value`**, and a tokio runtime awaits whole batches while it schedules others, with the stream pool replacing our hand rolled alternation. The per batch operation graph appears in Fig 11.2, and the alpha label from an earlier chapter still applies to the machinery beneath it:

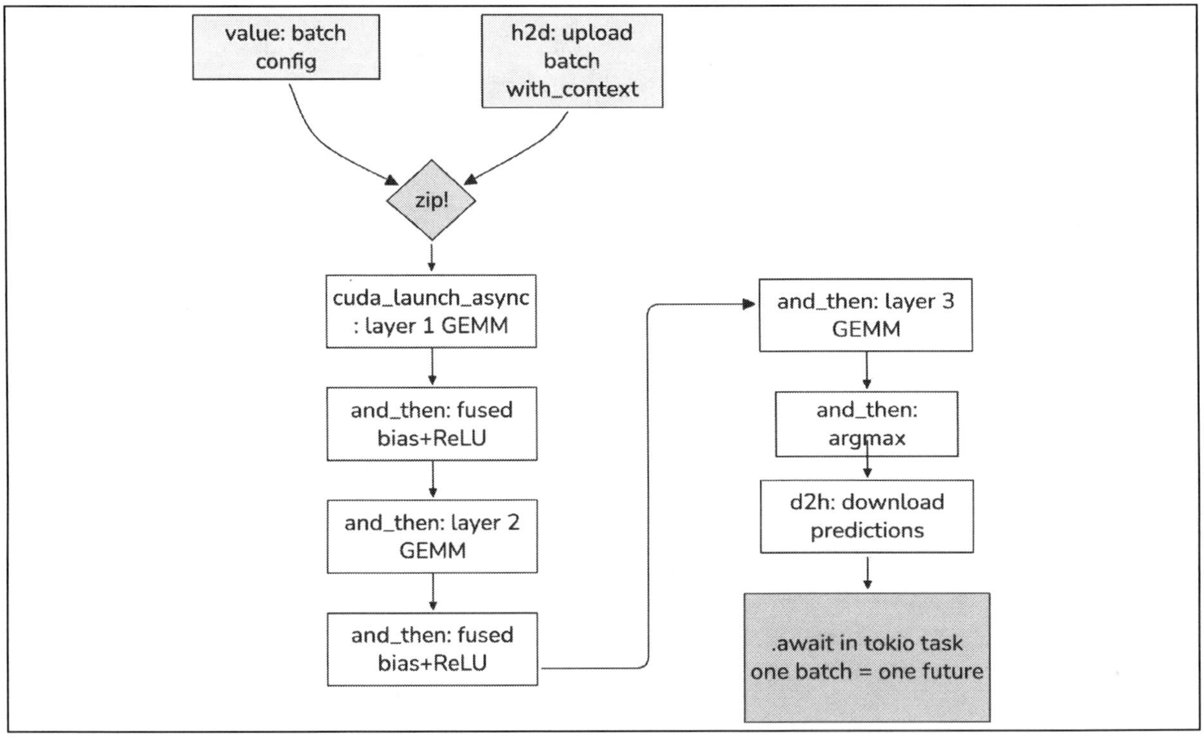

Fig 11.2: One Batch as DeviceOperation Graph

The graph form earns its keep at the boundaries. Because a batch is one awaitable value, the pipeline slots into a server that also awaits sockets and disk, and backpressure arrives through ordinary bounded channels rather than bespoke signaling. Our stream version needs careful manual sequencing to add such behavior, which is exactly the difference between scheduling by hand and describing work declaratively. When the cuda-oxide stack stabilizes, this chapter's design transfers onto it without a change of architecture, which is why we sketched both.

The choice between the two styles for a real deployment today follows the maturity labels we set earlier. Our hand scheduled version runs on stable, dependable crates and is the one we would ship this quarter, while the async graph runs on alpha machinery and is the one we would prototype beside it. Because both share the kernels, the wrapper, and the memory layout, the prototype costs little and the migration path stays open, which is how a careful team rides an evolving ecosystem without betting the product on it.

Measuring Result

Protocol and Fair Baselines

The measurement follows the book's settled protocol. The correctness gate compares one full batch against a CPU forward pass within relative tolerance before any timing, with the tolerance reasoning inherited straight from an earlier chapter. The throughput run processes all 64 batches and reports samples per second from wall clock, with event timings recorded per stage for the breakdown. We will run three configurations identically, namely our serial baseline on one stream, our overlapped pipeline on two, and an equivalent CuPy implementation whose stages call the same cuBLAS through Python. Twenty iterations run after a warm up, over the same data everywhere. Not a word of this paragraph is new policy, and its familiarity is deliberate, because a measurement protocol only earns trust through unvaried repetition across every experiment it touches.

The fairness rules from an earlier chapter apply unchanged to the baselines. The serial configuration uses the same pinned buffers, the same kernels, the same wrapper, and one stream, so overlap is again the only variable. The CuPy configuration receives the same courtesy in reverse, with its arrays preallocated, its kernels warmed, and its timing excluding import and setup, because a Python comparison that measures interpreter startup would flatter Rust dishonestly. The numbers below deserve trust precisely because the deck is not stacked.

Reading Numbers

We will now run **`cargo run -p mlp_pipeline`**, and our reference machine reports:

```
correctness: batch 0 matches CPU forward pass (max rel err 2.1e-6)

serial (1 stream):        4.41 M samples/s     14.9 ms total
```

```
overlapped (2 streams):   6.02 M samples/s    10.9 ms total
Python + CuPy:            2.96 M samples/s    22.1 ms total
first-batch latency:      0.24 ms
```

The ordering tells the story we have earned. The overlap buys roughly a third over serial, less than the near doubling of an earlier chapter because this pipeline computes more per transferred byte, so there is less idle transfer time to hide. The CuPy version trails at roughly half the Rust throughput, and the gap is pure per call dispatch overhead multiplied across eight operations and 64 batches, the small shapes edge we measured earlier. At tenfold larger batches, the same programs converge, and honesty requires saying so. The practical reading is that Rust's orchestration advantage concentrates exactly where production inference tends to live, in modest batches under latency budgets, rather than in the offline bulk runs where any language does fine.

The table turns into bars in Fig 11.3, and the breakdown from the event timings explains their heights. In the serial run, the upload consumes roughly half of each batch's turn, the three GEMMs take most of the rest, and the fused kernels and the download barely register on the axis at all. The overlapped run hides nearly the whole upload under the previous batch's compute, which is where the third of throughput came from, and the residual gap to perfect overlap is the first batch's unhidden upload plus scheduling slack:

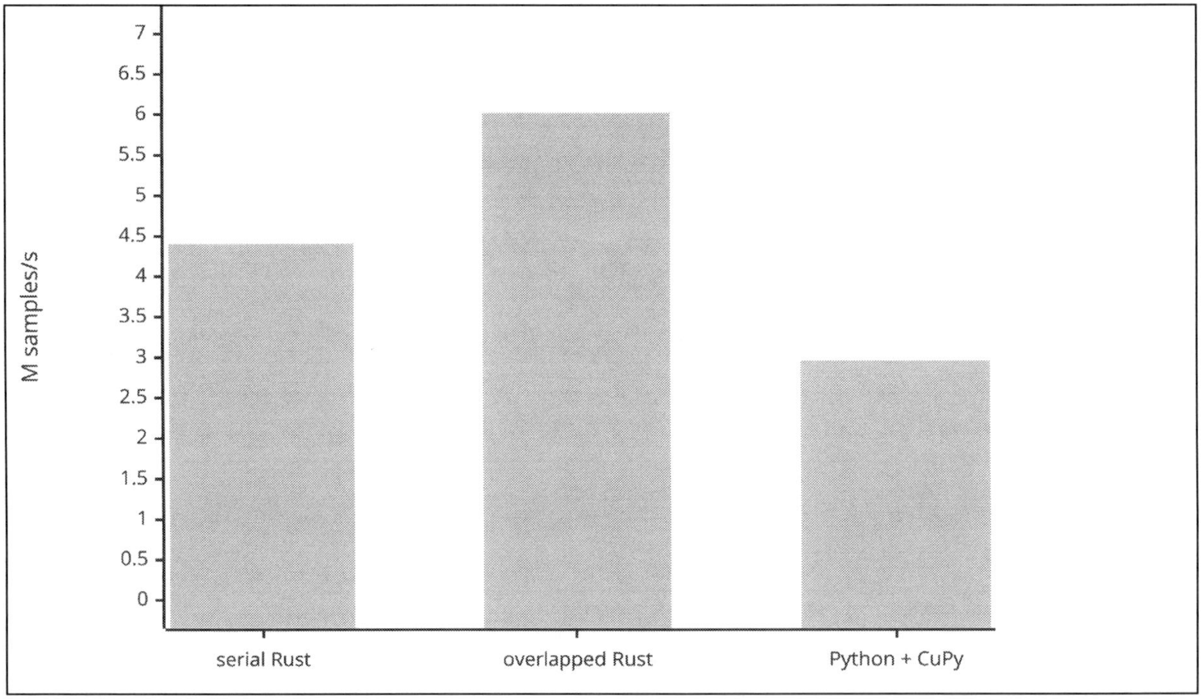

Fig 11.3: Capstone Throughput by Configuration

The throughput figure is not the only number a production system watch. The first predictions emerge after one batch traverses the pipeline, roughly a quarter of a millisecond on our machine, and the overlapped design holds that latency steady while throughput scales, since batches do not queue behind an idle bus. A single giant batch would post better samples per second and a hundredfold worse first result. The dial from the batching section is exactly this trade, now with numbers attached to both ends, and a service level agreement is usually what turns the dial in practice, since a promise of predictions within a millisecond constrains the batch size before throughput gets a vote.

The capstone closes the loop this book opened earlier. A complete GPU application, data handling through prediction, now runs in Rust with custom kernels where fusion pays, libraries where their shapes rule, overlap keeping every engine fed, and types guarding every seam we could give them. The Python comparison behaved exactly as the scoreboard predicted, competitive inside libraries and behind on orchestration, and the correctness gate held every configuration to the same standard before a single throughput number earned mention. At no point did the capstone require heroics, which is the strongest recommendation a technology stack can receive. One chapter remains, because every number we have reported deserves the scrutiny of real profilers, and chapter 12 teaches the tools that keep us honest at scale. Our claims about overlap, about hidden uploads, and about dispatch overhead have so far rested on our own clocks, and the final chapter lets independent instruments either confirm them or teach us something better. Whichever way it lands, the outcome improves the book's argument, which is the comfortable position that honest measurement always buys.

CHAPTER 12

PROVING PERFORMANCE

In this final chapter, we stop trusting ourselves and start trusting instruments. Every number this book has reported came from timers we wrote, which is a fine beginning and an incomplete practice, because timers reveal how long and never why. The NVIDIA profilers open the why, and they work on our Rust binaries without a single accommodation, since Nsight Systems, Nsight Compute, and compute-sanitizer all operate at the CUDA driver level where language has already disappeared. Our own workspace members supply every specimen this chapter dissects.

We will capture a whole application timeline and see the overlap of an earlier chapter with our eyes, interrogate a single kernel until it confesses its bottleneck, catch a planted race that a thousand test runs would miss, and sweep launch configurations to retire our folklore about block sizes. Every specimen comes from our own workspace, so each finding lands on code we understand down to the line. The chapter closes with the benchmarking checklist the whole book has been quietly following, gathered at last into one referencable place. No new machinery gets built today, and everything already built gets understood more deeply, which is the correct final act for a practice minded book that has promised evidence over enthusiasm at every step.

Measure, Don't Guess

Loop and Its Variance

The method deserves stating once in full, because every tuning session in existence is this loop or a worse improvisation. We measure to find where time goes, form one hypothesis about one cause, change the single thing the hypothesis names, and measure again under identical conditions. A change without a hypothesis is a lottery ticket, and a hypothesis without a re-measurement is a superstition in the making. The transpose campaign of an earlier chapter walked this loop three times, and the cycle appears in Fig 12.1:

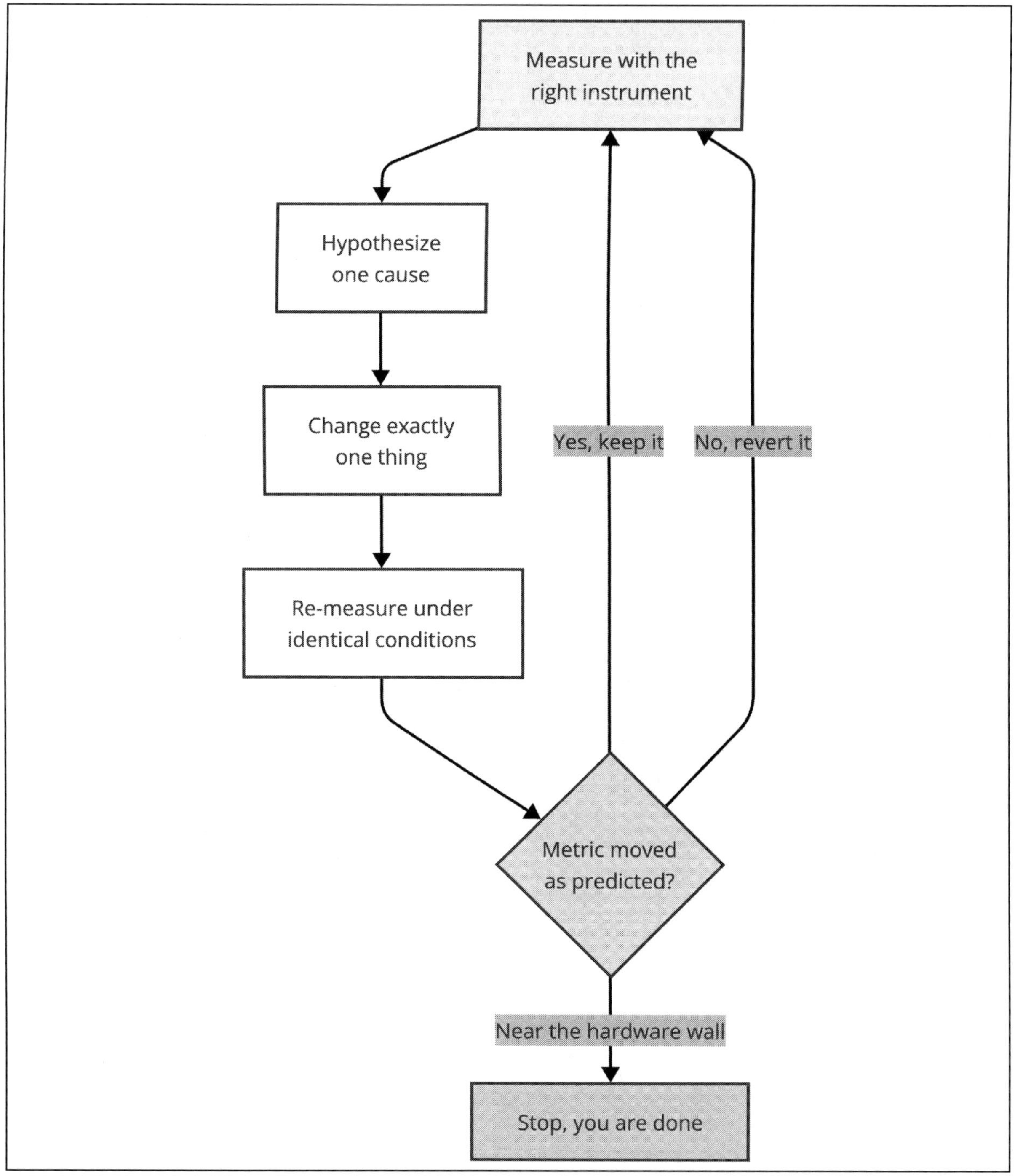

Fig 12.1: Optimizing Loop

The variance deserves respect before any conclusion. The GPU clocks move with temperature and power headroom, so the first iterations of any run flatter nothing, and single measurements lie in both directions. The warm up and twenty iteration average of our protocol absorb most of the noise, and a result worth acting on should hold up across two separate runs. When two configurations differ by less than run to run spread, the honest conclusion is a tie, however disappointing that feels after an afternoon of work. Our own scoreboard earlier called two such pair's ties for exactly this reason, and the discipline of conceding them is what makes the non-ties believable.

Three Instruments in Triage Order

We will rely on three instruments for the daily questions, the choice among them is a decision we can draw, and the order below is the order that saves the most evenings. When results are wrong, compute-sanitizer comes first, because tuning a broken kernel wastes everyone's time. When the application is slow but its kernels seem individually fine, Nsight Systems shows the timeline where gaps and serialization hide. When one kernel is the certified culprit, Nsight Compute dissects it against the hardware's own accounting. The triage appears in Fig 12.2:

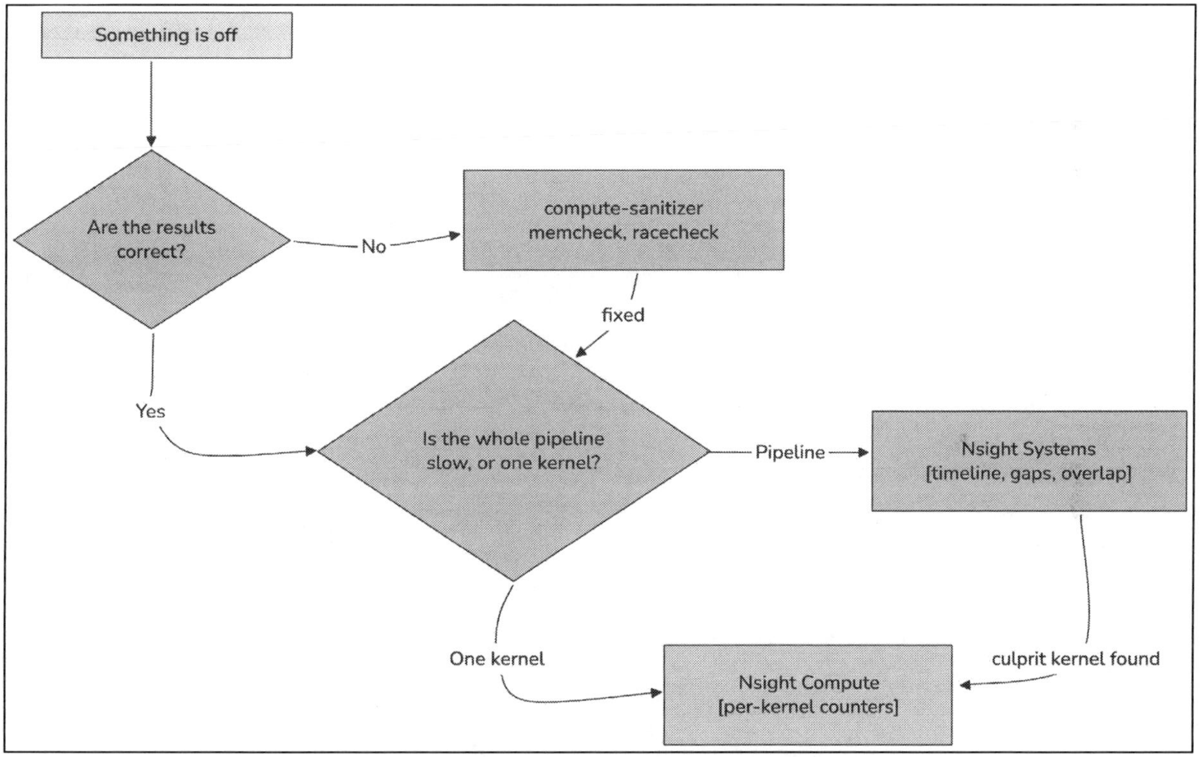

Fig 12.2: Choosing Instrument

The order matters as much as the assignments, and the arrows encode two lessons paid for in wasted evenings. A wrong result invalidates every timing taken beside it, so the sanitizer outranks both profilers whenever correctness is in doubt. And a slow pipeline with innocent kernels is common, since an earlier chapter showed how scheduling alone can double a runtime, which is why the wide lens precedes the microscope even when a particular kernel already looks suspicious. We resist the urge to zoom before we have surveyed.

Habits before First Capture

A pair of habits will make Rust programs pleasant to profile. We profile release builds only, since debug builds distort both host and kernel behavior beyond usefulness, and **`cargo build --release`** is cheap insurance. And we name our program's phases with NVTX ranges, the annotation API that Nsight tools display as labeled bands, which the nvtx crate exposes to Rust in a line per region. A timeline with named bands reads like our architecture diagram, while an unlabeled one reads like static. Five minutes of annotation before the first capture routinely saves an hour of squinting after it, which is the kind of exchange rate we accept without negotiation.

The tools install beside the toolkit and often with it. The apt packages from an earlier chapter's repository include nsight-systems and nsight-compute, the sanitizer ships inside the CUDA Toolkit itself, and all three carry current documentation at docs.nvidia.com. The viewer applications run happily on a workstation while the capture runs on a headless server, since reports are files that travel by ordinary copy, and this split matches how GPU boxes actually live in racks. The version skew between capture and viewer is the one recurring annoyance, and matched major versions avoid it.

Nsight Systems with Rust Binaries

Capturing Timeline

The Nsight Systems tool is the wide-angle lens, and one command captures everything. The nsys profile wrapper runs our binary while it records kernel launches, memory transfers, driver calls, CPU threads, and our NVTX ranges into a report file, and the companion viewer draws them as parallel timelines. The capture overhead stays low enough for production sized runs, so the numbers we profile remain the numbers we ship. The documentation at docs.nvidia.com covers every flag, and the defaults already serve well.

So here, we will capture our earlier pipeline in both of its configurations:

```
cargo build --release
nsys profile -o serial_run   ./target/release/stream_pipeline --serial
nsys profile -o overlap_run  ./target/release/stream_pipeline
```

The reports open in the graphical viewer, and a summary also prints straight to the terminal through nsys stats, which suits headless servers and quick checks. The tables rank kernels and transfers by total time, our kernels appear under their plain Rust names thanks to the naming fidelity an earlier chapter demonstrated, and in our serial capture the two memcpy rows own nearly the whole budget, which is the argument of an earlier chapter restated by an instrument that has never read this book.

The table below is worth reading slowly once, because its three columns of percentage, time, and instance count answer the three first questions of any investigation, namely what dominates, by how much, and how often it ran:

```
nsys stats serial_run.nsys-rep
```

```
** CUDA GPU Trace Summary (serial_run):
Time (%)  Total Time  Instances  Operation
--------  ----------  ---------  -------------------------
    46.9     21.4 ms         16  [CUDA memcpy Host-to-Device]
    45.8     20.9 ms         16  [CUDA memcpy Device-to-Host]
     5.2      2.4 ms         16  brighten
```

Reading Staircases and Gaps

The two reports settle an earlier chapter's claims visually. The serial capture shows the staircase we predicted, one row for compute and one per copy direction taking strict turns, with the GPU idle between steps. The overlapped capture shows the copy rows running under the compute row, the staircase compressed into overlapping shingles, and the wall clock shorter by exactly the ratio our events reported. To see the same truth from an independent instrument is the point, since our own timers could share our own blind spots.

The most valuable feature of the timeline is what it shows between kernels. Any gaps on the GPU rows mean the device waited for the host, and their usual causes are pageable transfers sneaking into an async design, synchronizations placed too eagerly, or launch overhead dominating tiny kernels. Our **`mlp_pipeline`** capture shows a clean weave with one honest flaw, the unhidden first upload from chapter 11's measurement. A profiler that confirms an expected flaw earns trust for the day it reveals an unexpected one.

One habit multiplies the value of every capture we ever take, namely keeping the report files beside the code they measured. A capture from last month turns a vague sense that things got slower into a diff between two timelines, with the regression's first appearance bracketed by commits, and the archaeology takes minutes instead of afternoons. The report files are small, our repository already versions everything else about the experiment, and future us will be grateful in direct proportion to how mechanical we make the filing.

Nsight Compute on Rust Kernels

Interrogating One Kernel

The Nsight Compute tool is the microscope, and it replays one kernel until every hardware counter has spoken. The ncu command below profiles our tiled GEMM inside **gemm_bench**, and the flag selects the kernel by name, which works because our Rust kernel names survive into PTX exactly as an earlier chapter showed. The replay makes runs slow, so we point it at one kernel at a time rather than at whole applications, the division of labor Fig 12.2 assigned.

We will now interrogate the kernel:

```
ncu -k gemm_tiled --set full ./target/release/gemm_bench
```

The relevant sections of the reply condense to a few telling lines:

```
Section: GPU Speed Of Light Throughput
    Compute (SM) Throughput             14.6 %
    Memory Throughput                   41.2 %
Section: Occupancy
    Theoretical Occupancy               66.7 %
    Achieved Occupancy                  61.9 %
    Limiter                             Shared Memory Per Block
Section: Launch Statistics
    Registers Per Thread                38
    Block Size                          1,024
```

Reading Report

We will give three sections of the report our daily attention. The speed of light summary states what fraction of the device's compute and memory ceilings the kernel reached, and it settles the first question of any tuning session, namely which wall we are near. The occupancy section reports how many warps each SM hosted against capacity, with the limiter named, whether registers, shared memory, or block slots. The launch statistics echo an earlier chapter's arithmetic back at us with the hardware's own accounting, and disagreements there have embarrassed many launch calculations.

Our tiled GEMM reads exactly as an earlier chapter diagnosed. The report shows respectable memory utilization, modest compute utilization, and occupancy limited by shared memory per block, which is the signature of a kernel that traded bandwidth for reuse and stopped before register blocking. The output effectively lists an earlier chapter's deliberately unclimbed ladder, and a professional could take this one screen and know precisely which optimization to attempt next. A report that names the next experiment is the whole value proposition of the microscope.

The report also settles an earlier chapter's warning about registers. A per thread register figure appears in the launch statistics, and when it climbs, occupancy falls in discrete steps as the SM register file divides among fewer warps, and heavy spills appear as local memory traffic in the memory tables. On the Rust side, the levers are the familiar ones, namely smaller kernels, fewer live temporaries, and the launch bounds options the kernel attributes accept. The source view can even map metrics onto lines when builds carry line information.

A calibration exercise makes the microscope familiar before a crisis demands it, and we recommend performing it once this week while the workspace is fresh. We profile the naive GEMM beside the tiled one and predict the differences before opening the reports, expecting the naive kernel to show saturated memory throughput with idle compute and the tiled kernel to show our measured shift. When the counters confirm a prediction we made from understanding, the tool stops feeling like an oracle and starts feeling like a colleague, which is the correct relationship to have with an instrument.

Correctness Tooling

Racecheck on Planted Bug

The compute-sanitizer utility is the tool we hope never fires, and we will make it fire on purpose. Its memcheck tool catches invalid addresses and out of bounds accesses, its racecheck tool watches shared memory for the exact hazards an earlier chapter warned about, and both run our binaries unmodified. The experiment plants the bug we theorized about, a scan kernel with the second barrier deleted, which passes its unit test on our machine every single time. This is precisely the deletion that an earlier chapter warned usually works, and the phrase usually works is the most dangerous phrase in parallel programming.

We will then let the instrument see what testing cannot:

```
compute-sanitizer --tool racecheck ./target/release/coop_lab
```

The instrument convicts the kernel on the first run:

```
========= ERROR: Race reported between Write access at
scan_inclusive+0x2f0
=========     and Read access at scan_inclusive+0x1a8 [4 bytes]
=========     in block-shared memory
========= RACECHECK SUMMARY: 1 hazard displayed (1 error, 0 warnings)
```

The report names the kernel, the shared address, and both conflicting accesses, and the bug that survived a thousand green tests dies in one instrumented run. The practice this suggests is cheap and permanent, namely a sanitizer pass in continuous integration for every kernel bearing project, slow but rare, and it catches the schedule dependent bugs before hardware variety does. The tool also validates our clean kernels, and a quiet racecheck over an earlier chapter's real reductions and scans is the certificate our SAFETY comments claimed.

Memcheck in 30 Seconds

The memcheck tool deserves its own thirty seconds. An off by one in a launch calculation, the classic overhang bug from an earlier chapter with the guard forgotten, produces silent corruption at worst and a hard crash at best, and memcheck converts both into a precise report naming the kernel, the address, and the access width. One command runs it, and its clean output over the whole workspace is one more certificate our chapters earned quietly along the way.

A reasonable question is what these instruments add in a language whose whole sales pitch is safety, and the answer keeps our claims calibrated. The borrow checker never saw our shared memory phases or our raw output pointers, as an earlier chapter admitted openly, so the sanitizer audits exactly the regions our **`unsafe`** blocks marked. The two systems compose rather than compete, with the type system shrinking the territory and the instrument patrolling what remains, and together they cover more ground than either alone ever could.

Controlling Tuning Levers

Block Size Sweep

The block size folklore from an earlier chapter finally faces data. Our sweep runs the tiled transpose and the sequential reduction at every block shape from 64 to 1024 threads, twenty timed iterations each under the settled protocol, and the results land close enough to folklore to be comforting and far enough to justify the sweep.

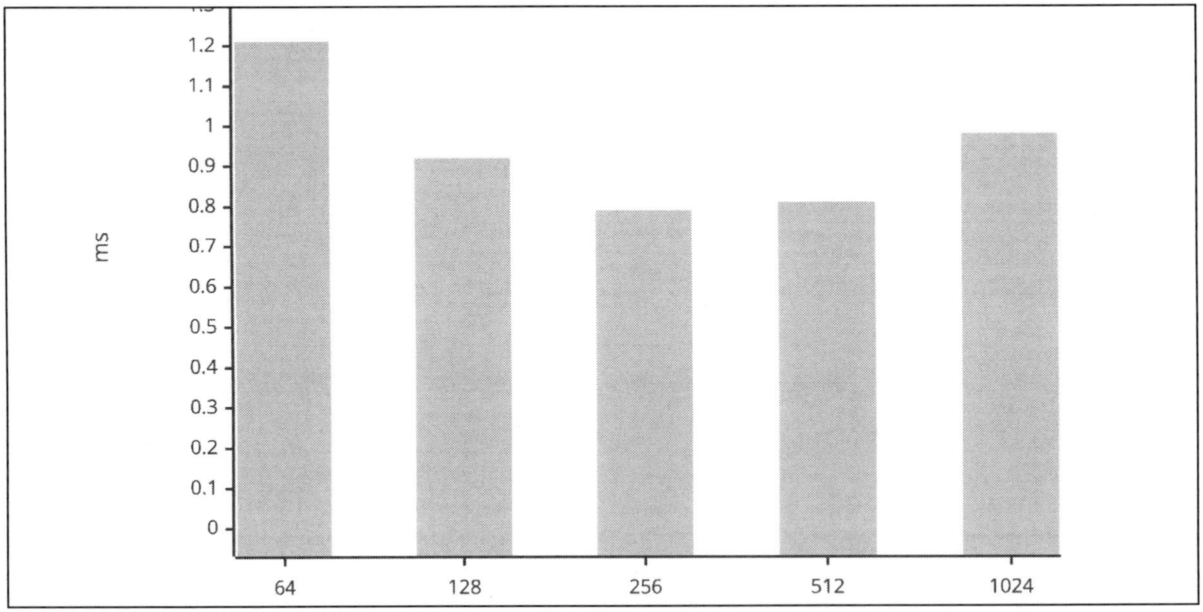

Fig 12.3: Block Size Sweep on Reduction Kernel

The reduction's curve appears in Fig 12.3, with 256 and 512 within noise of each other and both meaningfully ahead of the extremes:

The shape of the curve generalizes better than its peak. A small block starves SMs of resident warps and pays scheduling overhead per block, while a maximum size block reduces flexibility and can collide with register limits, so the broad middle wins on most kernels and most hardware. The sweep costs minutes and removes the question forever for a given kernel, which is why a measurement beats an occupancy calculator consulted in the abstract. Every project in our workspace can adopt the sweep harness with a loop around numbers it already produces.

The transpose sweep, which we omit for space, tells the same story with one instructive wrinkle, since its two-dimensional blocks tie the sweep to tile geometry and the 32 by 32 shape wins partly because it matches the tile the kernel was designed around. The lesson generalizes gently, namely that launch shape and algorithm shape tune together rather than separately, and a sweep that varies one while holding the other still answers only half the question. Our harness therefore records both dimensions in its output rows.

Checklist and Closing Inventory

A final word protects the loop from its own enthusiasm. The levers worth pulling are the ones instruments point at, and the reports rank them for us, while folklore suggests unrolls, caches, and exotic flags in whatever order a forum thread once used. The rhythm of an earlier chapter holds, one change and one measurement, and any edit that fails to move its metric reverts regardless of how clever it felt. The optimization ends when the speed of light section says the relevant wall is near, not when ideas run out.

The benchmarking checklist gathers the book's scattered discipline into one place. We verify before timing, warm up before measuring, time twenty iterations with events for device work and wall clock for pipelines, hold every variable but one, pin memory when async paths matter, compile release, state the hardware and driver beside every number, and keep the harness in the repository so anyone can rerun it. None of these steps is clever, and their combination is what let this book publish numbers without flinching. The checklist rides in the repository as a plain file beside the code, because a discipline that lives in a document gets followed on the days when memory would have skipped it.

A quick inventory shows how far the workspace traveled. Our twelve members now span diagnostics, kernels in two toolchains, memory and cooperation laboratories, pipelines, benchmarks, a pricer, and a capstone application, and every one still builds and verifies with two commands on a fresh machine. The examples were never disposable, which was a promise from an earlier chapter, and the profiling harnesses from this chapter attach to all of them. Whoever extends this workspace next inherits instruments, baselines, and habits together, which is a better endowment than any single fast kernel could be.

Our toolbox is complete, and so is the argument. In the end, Rust joined CUDA without asking permission, wrote kernels that matched C++, called libraries at full speed, kept pace with Python's comfort while beating its orchestration, and wrapped the whole practice in types that made entire bug families unrepresentable. The experimental edges remain edges, and we labeled every one along the way. What this book set out to show is now proven where it matters, on hardware, under instruments, with the workspace as the witness. The rest is workloads, and those are yours to bring. Whatever shape they take, the path through them is the one we have walked twelve times now, namely a verified baseline, one measured change at a time, honest labels on experimental ground, and instruments trusted over instincts. We would be glad to hear where the road leads, because a growing community of practitioners is exactly what this young ecosystem needs next, and every workspace like ours widens the pavement a little for whoever follows.

Index

H

I

K

L

M

N

O

P

Q

R

S

T

U

V

W

X

Epilogue

Just twelve chapters ago, we were pondering whether Rust could step into the world of GPU computing and feel right at home. The reply is now saved in the workspace on your machine.

What we've got here is a device query that gave us the lowdown on the hardware, a planner that turned thread hierarchies from vocabulary into arithmetic, and kernels written in pure Rust that produced PTX indistinguishable from anything C++ ever emitted. It holds a transpose that taught us memory is the whole game, reductions and scans that made cooperation safe through discipline rather than luck, and pipelines where every engine on the card finally worked at once. It's got a matrix multiply that went from being 2% of the hardware's peak to being pretty decent, and then met cuBLAS and learned humility. It uses a pricer that's been checked against a formula, and an application that we can defend line by line because we measured it using NVIDIA's own instruments.

So, did Rusty get the position? As far as our records go, that's what they say. When it comes to kernels, the language didn't change anything about speed, but it did change everything about confidence, since the same PTX now comes with whole families of bugs that can't be represented. When it comes to libraries, Rust is right up there with Python, calling them at full speed and working around them even faster. When it comes to the ecosystem, it's best to be honest. One toolchain wants a pinned nightly, another wears an alpha label its own authors insist upon, and the road still has gravel patches that C++ paved over years ago. We drove it anyway and we made it there.

What happens next is down to the projects and us. The Rust GPU ecosystem is still pretty new, so if you contribute a fix, report a bug, or share a benchmark from your hardware, it can really make a difference. The workspace you built is a great tool for exactly that kind of contribution. It's worth extending it. The profilers should be pointed at your own workloads. If you swap our synthetic weights for your real models and our uniform bytes for your actual data, you'll see which conclusions stand up to your problems. The benchmarking checklist from the final chapter will make sure the results are trustworthy when no one's watching.

And don't forget to keep up the habit of verify → change one thing → measure again → label the experimental loop. The GPU rewards that discipline with performance, and Rust rewards it with certainty, and the two rewards compound in a way that neither language nor hardware delivers alone. In the future, we'll have stabilized compilers, better safety models and libraries created by people who read chapters like ours and decided to fill the gaps. Maybe you're one of those people.

--Maris Fenlor

Thank You

Made in the USA
Coppell, TX
05 November 2026

11299172R00092